THE JEWS IN AMERICA

The IN AMERICA *Series*

THE JEWS IN AMERICA

FRANCES BUTWIN

Published by
Lerner Publications Company
Minneapolis, Minnesota

ACKNOWLEDGMENTS

The illustrations are reproduced through the courtesy of: p. 6, Hispanic Society of America, New York; pp. 8, 10, 14, 28 (bottom), 31, 32, 34, 37, 38, 49, 50, 51, 57, 58. 59 (top), 64 (left), 73, 78, 81, 82, 83 (top right and bottom), 89, 93, 94 (top left), 96, 97 (top and bottom right), 98 (top), Independent Picture Service; p. 11, Bibliotheque Nationale, Service Photographie; p. 12, Museo Nacional del Prado, Madrid; pp. 16, 19, 21, 22, Jewish Publication Society of America; pp. 17, 20, 59 (bottom), 88, Library of Congress; p. 25, Chicago Historical Society, Photo by J. Sherwin Murphy; pp. 28 (top), 40, 41, 42, 43, 44, 72 (top left), 83 (top left), 92, 100, *Dictionary of American Portraits*, Dover Publications, Inc.; p. 36, California Palace of the Legion of Honor, Mildred Anna Williams Collection; p. 45, Hebrew Union College—Jewish Institute of Religion; pp. 52, 53, 54, 55, 56, *Jewish Daily Forward*; pp. 60, 76, Museum of the City of New York, Jacob A. Riis Collection; pp. 61, 62 (top), 67, New York Public Library; pp. 62 (bottom), 64 (right), 65, International Ladies Garment Workers' Union; pp. 63, 71, Museum of the City of New York, Byron Collection; p. 66, Simon and Schuster; p. 69, Harvard University Press; pp. 72 (top right), 84, Yivo Institute for Jewish Research; p. 72 (bottom), Warner Brothers; p. 73, Mandelstam Photo Service; p. 75, B. Manischewitz Company; p. 77, Community Service Society Archives; p. 79 (left), Detroit Tigers; p. 79 (right), Los Angeles Dodgers; p. 86, University of Pittsburgh; p. 87, Rutgers News Service, photo by Francis J. Higgins; p. 94 (top right and bottom right), United Artists Corporation; p. 94 (bottom left), ABC Television; p. 97 (bottom left), National Broadcasting Company; p. 98 (bottom), New York Philharmonic; p. 99, Marlborough-Gerson Gallery, New York, Photo by Alice Rewald; p. 101, Mr. and Mrs. James Schramm, Burlington, Iowa; p. 102, Metro-Goldwyn-Mayer, Inc.; p. 103, D. J. Davies; p. 104, Viking Press, Photo by Jeff Lowenthal; p. 105, Israel Zamir; p. 106, New York Public Library, Astor, Lenox and Tilden Foundations.

The Library of Congress cataloged the
original printing of this title as follows:

Butwin, Frances.
    The Jews in America. Minneapolis, Lerner Publications Co.
[1969]

    107 p. illus., facsims., map, ports. 24 cm. (The In America Series)

    Traces the history of the Jews in the United States and their role in the political, cultural, and industrial development of the country. Also discusses the causes and origins of anti-semitism.

    1. Jews in the United States—Juvenile literature. [1. Jews in the United States] I. Title.

E184.J5B83   301.451'924'073   68-31501
ISBN 0-8225-0217-8   MARC
                                                     A C

International Standard Book Number: 0-8225-0217-8
Library of Congress Catalog Card Number: 68-31501

Second Printing 1969
Third Printing 1970
Fourth Printing 1971
Fifth Printing 1974

...CONTENTS...

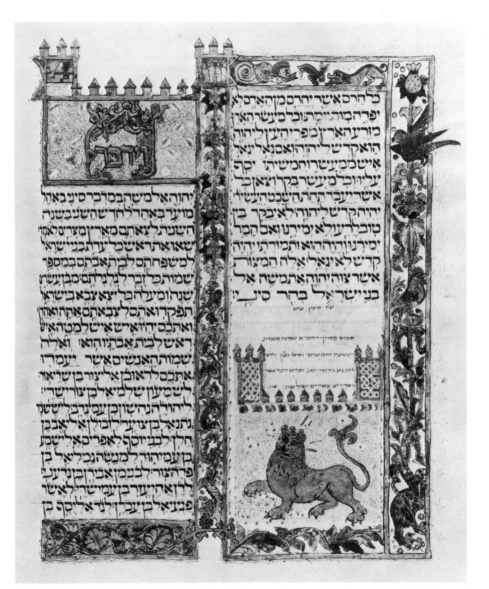

Page from a Hebrew Bible. Toledo, Spain, 1491. A year later, Ferdinand and Isabella completed the Christian reconquest of Spain and expelled the Jews. From Spain the Jews went to the Near East, The Netherlands, and the Americas.

PART I

The Jews in Early America

1. *The Link with Columbus*

Though the first group of Jews to settle in the American colonies came to New Amsterdam in 1654, the history of the Jews in America begins with the discovery of America itself.

Christopher Columbus wrote in his diary: "After the Spanish monarchs had banished all the Jews from their kingdoms and territories, in the same month they gave me the order to undertake with sufficient men my voyage of discovery to the Indies." Was this mere coincidence, or was Columbus aware of a link between the banishment of the Jews and the order to undertake a voyage of discovery? We know that after Columbus had been turned down by the King of Portugal, he appealed to King Ferdinand and Queen Isabella of Spain for men, money, and ships, and that the Spanish monarchs for several years refused his request. Spain was not yet a sea power. The King and Queen, who by their marriage had united the provinces of Aragon and Castile in the north, were busy driving the Moors out of southern Spain, Christianizing their own people, and consolidating their kingdom. They had neither the time nor the money to risk on a venture such as Columbus proposed — to find a route east by sailing west.

But in the year 1492 two important events took place. In January, Granada, the last stronghold of the Moors in southern Spain, fell. At the end of March the King and Queen signed an order that all the Jews who wouldn't convert to Christianity leave within four months, and that their wealth and property be left to the Crown. At last Queen

Columbus at the court of Queen Isabella of Spain.

Isabella had the money—and the inclination—to listen to the sailor from Genoa. She conferred on him the title of Admiral and gave him three ships and 90 men for his voyage of discovery. Columbus sailed with the *Nina*, the *Pinta*, and the *Santa Maria*, on August 3, 1492, exactly one day after the final expulsion of the Jews from Spain.

2. *The Golden Age in Spain*

Among the 90 men who set out with Columbus were five Jews who had been converted to Christianity. The converts were officially called *conversos* or New Christians, but in popular speech they were known as *Marranos*. Two of the Marranos with Columbus, Bernal and Marco, were physicians, and a third, Luis de Torres, was his interpreter. Columbus sent the first reports of his discoveries to two of the Queen's ministers who had pleaded his cause and helped him with their own money—Luis Santangel and Gabriel Sanchez. These men were also Marranos.

Though many Marranos held high places at the Spanish Court and were as wealthy and proud as any Spanish grandee, their life was an uneasy one. The very word Marrano was a term of contempt. It meant "pig" in Spanish. Because the Marranos had been converted against their will, they still practiced their own religion in secret. They were under constant suspicion of heresy and often underwent questioning and torture. No wonder so many of them risked their lives and fortunes to follow the explorers to the New World.

To understand why some Jews were converted and why the majority who refused conversion — between 200,000 and 300,000 — were expelled in 1492, we have to go back to what is known as the Golden Age of the Jews in Spain.

This Golden Age was a period of freedom, prosperity, and intellectual development for the Jews. It began with the conquest of southern Spain by the Moors in the eighth century and lasted into the fourteenth century — roughly about 600 years. The Moors, who came from North Africa, were an Arab people of the Moslem religion. They had developed a brilliant civilization, noted for its literature and art and the sciences of medicine, astronomy, and mathematics. They were tolerant toward the Jews, who had developed their own culture in Babylonia and North Africa. After the Moorish conquest of southern Spain in 711, great numbers of Jews flocked to Cordoba and other cities where they established their own communities and academies of learning. These academies produced religious as well as secular scholars, philosophers, poets, doctors, and linguists. Jewish scholars translated books from Hebrew, Greek, and Arabic into Latin, which later Christian scholars found useful. To this age belongs Moses Maimonides (1135-1204) who, like many great men, combined several fields of knowledge. He was a doctor of medicine, an astronomer, a Biblical scholar, and a philosopher. His most famous book, *A Guide for the Perplexed,* wove religion, philosophy, and the natural sciences into a harmonious whole, as a guide of conduct for enlightened man. His was a humanist concept of life far in advance of his day.

Trade flourished, too, as it usually does in an enlightened age when men exchange not only ideas but material goods. The Spanish cities made famous by the Moors, with the help of the Jews, still have a splendid ring in our ears — Cordoba, Malaga, Seville, Granada. The Moorish temples and palaces and Jewish synagogues, some of which later became Christian churches, had an influence on the architecture and art of Spain which persists to this day.

In the eleventh century the northern provinces of Spain united under Christian rulers and began to drive the Moors out of the Iberian Peninsula. In the savage wars that followed the Jews were caught

Moses Maimonides (1135-1204) left Cordoba at the age of 13, when fanatical Moslems — the Almohades — invaded the city. In about 1165 his family settled in Cairo where he later became physician in the court of the sultan Saladin. Maimonides's philosophical works have influenced both Jewish and Christian thought.

between two forces — that of Islam and Christianity. Some Jews went back to North Africa, among them Maimonides with his family. Others went to northern Spain where at first the Christian rulers welcomed them. Both Spain and Portugal were glad to utilize their skills in commerce and the sciences. Prince Henry the Navigator of Portugal employed the cartographer, Judah Cresques, who became known as "the map Jew," or the "compass Jew." Other Jews and Marranos compiled astronomical tables and invented the perpetual almanac, which proved of great use in the voyages of exploration.

But the Golden Age dimmed as the Catholic Church grew in power and began to overshadow the state. The Dominican Order, which controlled the Church in Spain, was more concerned with the conversion of non-believers than with the advancement of science. Jews who wouldn't accept conversion were threatened with loss of their property and positions in commerce, the government, and the army. Under pressure many converted. These were the New Christians, or in popular language, the Marranos.

But the act of baptism wasn't enough. The Church set up a tribunal, or court, which brought to trial any New Christians who were not zealous enough in following the new faith. This tribunal was called The Inquisition or Holy Office, with a Grand Inquisitor at its head.

It performed an elaborate ritual which culminated with torture to make the accused confess their "heresy." Thousands of victims were burned at the stake. The Spanish Inquisition sought out not only the Marranos, but people of other faiths, as well as Christians suspected of heresy. It followed its victims to the New World, and lasted in one form or another until almost the time of the French Revolution.

At the time of Columbus the Grand Inquisitor was Tomas de Torquemada, Queen Isabella's confessor, and it was he who prevailed upon the King and Queen to sign the order which in the words of Columbus, "banished all the Jews from their kingdoms and territories."

3. *The Sephardim and Ashkenazim*

The Jews who were driven from Spain, and soon after that from Portugal, fanned out over central and northern Europe, joining Jewish settlements which already existed or forming new ones. The country that proved most hospitable was Holland, which was to become a haven for religious and political dissenters of all kinds, including the English Puritans. The Netherlands was fighting for its own in-

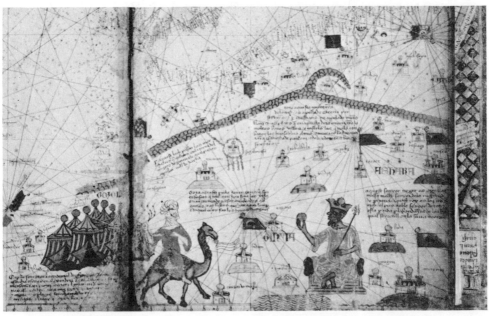

Detail from a map of the world by Judah Cresques, cartographer to Henry the Navigator (1394-1460), Prince of Portugal.

A medieval Inquisition conducted by Dominicans. Two heretics (lower right) are about to be burned at the stake. The pope established the Inquisition in 1231, in order to weed out unbelievers. In 1478 Ferdinand and Isabella set up their own Inquisition to seek and punish converted Jews and Moors suspected of backsliding. The papacy had little control over the Spanish Inquisition and generally disapproved of it.

dependence from Spain, and perhaps for that reason welcomed exiles from that country. Besides, the Jews had skills and aptitudes that were useful to a nation which, like Holland, was trying to develop as a mercantile and colonial power. In Amsterdam there grew up a large and influential Jewish community which was to have some bearing on the settlement of the Jews in America.

Wherever the Jews from the Iberian Peninsula went they carried with them not only their religious heritage, but their Spanish and Portuguese language and culture. These Jews were called Sephardim, or Sephardic Jews, from the Hebrew name for Spain, *Sepharad*. They are distinguished from another branch of the Jewish people, the Ashkenazim, a word derived from the Hebrew name for Germany — *Ashkenaz*. These Jews had settled in Germany in the early Middle Ages and developed a German-Jewish culture and language. In time the term Ashkenazim, or Ashkenazic Jews, came to include also the Polish, Russian, and other East European Jews. All of them had the same religion, but the rituals differed somewhat. Then, too, the Sephardim considered themselves to be of an older and more patrician stock than the Ashkenazim and tended to keep themselves aloof. In America they were "the first settlers."

4. *New Amsterdam*

In September 1654, a French privateer, the *St. Charles*, tied up at a wharf in New Amsterdam at the tip of Manhattan Island. Aboard the *St. Charles* was a group of 23 Jews — men, women, and children — tired, bedraggled, and penniless but with plenty of spirit. They needed spirit, for the Governor of New Netherland refused them permission to land. Suppose he let them in, Peter Stuyvesant stormed, he would soon have to let in the papists, the Quakers, the Lutherans. Stuyvesant was known for his harsh, dictatorial methods and his strict adherence to the Dutch Reformed Church. In spite of the liberal policies of his employers, the Dutch West India Company, he kept tight control of his own little colony. His position was far from secure. His settlement was isolated in the New World, surrounded on all sides by the British, and by the Swedes in Delaware, with the only other Dutch settlement, Fort Orange, far up the Hudson River to the north. The Dutch had little agriculture. Their chief occupation was fur trading with the Indians.

How did the small band of Jews happen to come to this little Dutch outpost in North America, and where had they come from?

They were Sephardic Jews of Portuguese descent, but they had come from Recife (City of Reefs) in Brazil, a town now called Pernambuco. Brazil had been colonized by Portugal in the sixteenth century, and some Marranos had come there with the Portuguese explorers and settlers. Under Portuguese rule they could not practice their own religion. But when Holland captured some cities in Brazil and Guiana, the Marranos returned to their own faith. In 1621 the Dutch West India Company was formed in Amsterdam and some of the directors and stockholders were Jews. The Dutch took Recife in 1631 and among

The first group of Jews to settle in America came from
Brazil to New Amsterdam in 1654. Above, the city in 1670.

the shiploads of Dutch settlers were a number of Jews. They built a
synagogue and within 30 years had a community of 5,000 — more than
twice the number of Jews that came to the North American colonies
before the American Revolution.

When Recife was recaptured by the Portuguese in 1654, the Jews
were again set adrift. Many returned to Holland, some went to
Surinam (Dutch Guiana), others to Curacao, Jamaica, Barbados, and
other islands of the Caribbean. The little group on the *St. Charles*
headed north and reached New Amsterdam. They stayed on the ship
until the Dutch West India Company sent orders to Stuyvesant to let
them land. He submitted with bad grace, warning the newcomers that
they must not become a burden on the colony. They were allowed to
trade with the Indians on the Hudson and Delaware, but were not
granted full burghers' rights. Their leader, Asser Levy, protested
when the Jews were made to pay a tax instead of being allowed to
serve in the militia. Another leader of the group was Jacob Barsimson
who had come on a ship called the *Perebom* (Peartree).

One of the first rights the Jews asked for was permission to buy a
plot of land for a cemetery. This was a pattern to be repeated in each
new settlement. Long before they made plans for a house of worship,
the Jews wanted a piece of ground in which to bury their dead. As a
result the history of old settlers can often be traced not from buildings
which burn down or are demolished, but from sunken old gravestones.

Ten years later, in 1664, King Charles II of England sent his fleet
to capture New Amsterdam and claim the land for England. He re-
named the city New York, in honor of his brother, the Duke of York.
It seems appropriate that the first American town in which a group of

14

Jews settled came to have the largest Jewish population of any city in America, and indeed in the world.

5. *Newport, Rhode Island*

The second Jewish settlement in the American colonies was in Newport, Rhode Island. A small group of Jews came to Newport from Holland in 1658; others came later from South America, the West Indies, and from Lisbon, Portugal. By the time of the American Revolution, Newport had the largest Jewish community in America.

Jews came to the American colonies for the same reasons other colonists came — to seek political and religious freedom, and economic opportunity. Political rights, such as the right to vote, to hold office, and to serve in the militia, were granted to Jews only here and there in the colonies; in most places they were denied. Jews were considered "an alien nation," though they were not a nation at all, but came from many nations and spoke a number of languages. They had their religion in common and the practice of their religion was not denied to them. In New England, especially, where the Puritans studied the Old Testament and gave their children such Biblical names as Nathaniel, Ezra, Ezekiel, Abigail, and Rachel, the Jews were looked upon with respect. But the Puritans' theology had a strange twist to it. They believed in the Second Coming of Christ, when the dead would arise, a final judgment take place, and the millenium or new age would dawn. But they believed that before this Second Coming, the conversion of all the Jews would have to take place. The Puritans didn't try to force this conversion, but they awaited it with hope.

A few conversions took place. The American colonies, like the mother country, England, at first excluded Jews from colleges. (England did not grant degrees to Jews until 1871.) The first Jew to get a degree from Harvard was Judah Monis, who had come from Italy. He received an M.A. degree from Harvard in 1720, but it appears that before he could get a teaching post he had to become a Christian. In March 1722, in an impressive ceremony, Judah Monis was baptized at College Hall, Cambridge, and was appointed Instructor in Hebrew. He taught Hebrew at Harvard until 1760 and published *A Grammar of the Hebrew Tongue,* the first Hebrew grammar to be published in

America. Though he belonged to the First Church at Cambridge and left a bequest in his will to the widows of poor clergymen, Judah Monis stuck to one tenet of his old faith. He always observed the seventh day as his Sabbath.

A more liberal attitude was taken in 1769 by the founders of Rhode Island College at Providence (later Brown University). The trustees provided for complete freedom of religion for all students and exempted Jewish students from attending Christian services. The college received gifts of money from Jewish merchants as far away as Charlestown, South Carolina. Aaron Lopez of Newport donated 10,000 feet of lumber.

Rhode Island had been founded in 1636 by Roger Williams, a young minister who believed in freedom of religion for everybody. That was one reason why the Jews came to Newport. Another reason was that Newport was a prominent seaport and commercial center. The Sephardic Jews who settled there had business connections in London and Amsterdam and soon built up trade with other American seaports. Early maps of Newport show Bellevue Avenue lined with shops owned by Jewish merchants of Spanish and Portuguese descent. The shipowners and traders had such names as Rivera, Lopez, Mendez, and Seixas. The most prominent among them was Aaron Lopez who came from Lisbon in 1752 and became one of the "merchant princes" of his day. He and his brother Moses owned ships which carried cargos

Aaron Lopez (1731-1782) settled in Newport in 1752. By 1776 he had a merchant fleet of 30 ships. When the British took Newport, Lopez moved to Leicester, Massachusetts. His commercial strength — and Newport's — was broken. He died in a carriage accident on his way back to Newport after the war.

Interior of the Touro synagogue, Newport, Rhode Island.

of goods to Europe and up and down the Atlantic coast. Letters from Charlestown merchants mention the exchange of such goods as rice, potatoes, "nutts," rum and molasses, and casks of red and white Lisbon wine. Jacob Rivera, in association with others, began to process spermaceti oil (whale oil) which was so important to American colonists in making candles and oil for lamps. By 1776 there were 1,200 Jews in Newport in a total population of 7,500.

Before they built a synagogue and appointed a rabbi, the Jews of Newport used to write to friends and relatives in Amsterdam and London for advice on religious matters in relation to births, marriages, deaths, and the observance of holidays. It took the letters so long to cross the ocean that they had to improvise their own rules. In 1763 the Jews of Newport built a synagogue which was designed in the Georgian style by Peter Harrison, an English architect. The Sephardic ritual was observed in this synagogue, which was named the Touro synagogue for its first officiating rabbi, Isaac Touro. It is the oldest synagogue in America still standing, and together with the Tuoro cemetery it has become a historic landmark of colonial America.

6. *Philadelphia*

The first Jews to appear in Pennsylvania came down from New Amsterdam to trade with the Indians along the Delaware River as early as 1655. "Israelites," as they were called, were considered a curiosity, on a par with the Indians. In fact, William Penn expressed the opinion, held by some colonists, that the American Indians were descended from the ten lost tribes of Israel. To the Jews who came to settle in his colony he granted religious freedom, but not full civil rights.

Early in the eighteenth century Lancaster, Pennsylvania, which was an important frontier post for the western fur trade, had a small Jewish community, with its own place of worship and a cemetery. In 1747 the Jews of Philadelphia held religious services in a rented room in Sterling Alley. Around that time there appeared an advertisement in Benjamin Franklin's *Pennsylvania Gazette* asking that sportsmen forebear from using the brick wall of the Jewish burying ground as a target for shooting practice. It further stated that anyone who reported these "sportsmen" would receive a reward of 20 shillings from the undersigned, Nathan Levy. This Nathan Levy, who had bought the burial plot, was a well-to-do merchant, a prominent citizen, and a member of Philadelphia society, who "played a very good violine" at a concert in the Music Hall of Philadelphia.

Not all the Jewish settlers in Pennsylvania owned burial plots or belonged to musical societies. Most of them were pack peddlers who went into the wilderness to barter with the Indians, exchanging a brass kettle, a gun, or a bottle of rum, for a bundle of deerskins. Others made a living as sutlers selling provisions to soldiers in the French and Indian wars. But the colonists who left records behind them in the form of business letters, newspaper notices, and wills must of necessity have been those who had business to transact by letter, wares to advertise in the papers, and money and silver plate to leave to their heirs.

One of the families that left such records was the Gratz family. Bernard Gratz was born in a town in Upper Silesia on the Polish-Prussian border in 1738, and left home as a young boy to seek his fortune in London. He arrived in Philadelphia in 1754. At first he worked as a clerk for another Philadelphia merchant, David Franks.

When he heard that his brother Michael was planning to come to America he wrote to him to bring from London about 20 silver watches, some "new-fashioned watch chains," 20 dozen women's shoes, and "a few dozen women's mittens in black worsted."

Within a few years the Gratz brothers were shipping to England cargos of raw furs, cattle, grain, and lumber, presumably in exchange for more silver watches and women's worsted mittens. This was the pattern of colonial trade — raw materials in exchange for manufactured goods. Soon England was imposing heavy duties on the export trade. In protest against the Stamp Act, which taxed all legal documents and ships' papers, the colonial merchants banded together to sign a non-importation agreement in Philadelphia in 1765, pledging themselves not to import goods from England until the Stamp Act was repealed. Among the signers of this agreement were Bernard and Michael Gratz.

The Jews of Philadelphia didn't start to plan a synagogue building until the 1770's. The synagogue was built on Cherry Street and dedicated in 1782 in the midst of the Revolutionary War. Its first rabbi was Gershom Mendez Seixas, who had been the rabbi of the New York congregation but had left at the time of the British occupation. This Cherry Street synagogue was used as a house of worship by Philadelphia Jews until 1825.

Michael Gratz (1740-1811) helped open up western lands for settlement and trade. With his brother Bernard he formed a land company with holdings in Ohio, Kentucky, Indiana, and Illinois. During the Revolution the Gratz brothers ran supplies through the British blockade.

Charlestown, South Carolina, in the early eighteenth century. Founded in 1670, it became the greatest Southern seaport in colonial America.

7. *Charlestown*

The first Jew to be mentioned in South Carolina history was an interpreter, and he remains anonymous. When Governor John Archdale published *A New Description of that Fertile and Pleasant Province of Carolina* (London, 1707) he wrote of a remarkable incident that happened in 1695. Some Yammassee Indians "going a Hunting, about 200 miles to the Southward," had captured four Indians near St. Augustine, Florida, and brought them to Charles Town, intending to sell them as slaves in Barbados or Jamaica. After interviewing the captives, the governor set them free. The Florida Indians, wrote the governor, "could speak *Spanish* and I had a *Jew* for an interpreter." This Jew may have been a former Marrano.

Charles Town (now Charleston) was a busy seaport and the largest and most cosmopolitan city in the South. It drew many Jews of Spanish descent who came from England and from the British possessions in the West Indies. Such names as Simon Vallentine, Jacob Mendis, Abraham Avilah are mentioned in early documents. They are described as "merchants," a term which applied not only to those in the shipping trade but to peddlers and shopkeepers. South Carolina had a liberal constitution which in its original draft promised freedom of worship to "Jews, Heathens," and others. The final draft didn't mention the Jews, but they enjoyed most of the privileges granted to other dissenters, among whom were the French Huguenots.

The first Jewish congregation in Charlestown was organized about 1749. It was called *Beth Elohim,* the House of God, and its services were conducted in the Sephardic ritual. It moved from place to place until 1794 when a synagogue was built which General Lafayette on a visit to the city is supposed to have admired. It was destroyed by fire in 1835. The present *Beth Elohim,* one of the oldest reform synagogues in America, stands on a plot of land which had been donated to the congregation by the heirs of Joseph Tobias, who served as the president of the first congregation.

The cemetery of *Beth Elohim,* the first Jewish congregation in Charlestown. Graves in the cemetery date from 1762.

The *hazan* or cantor of that earliest congregation was Isaac Da Costa, a merchant who had come from London in about 1740. Da Costa is said to have "moved in the best Charlestown circles," belonging to the Masons and the Palmetto Society. He did business with Aaron and Moses Lopez of Newport and carried on an extensive correspondence with them. In Newport, Isaac Da Costa met the Congregationalist minister, Ezra Stiles, who made a point of meeting cultivated Jews and discussing the Scriptures with them.

A shopkeeper's advertisement in the South Carolina *Gazette*, 1735.

Another New England clergyman, Hezekiah Smith, came to Charlestown in 1769 to raise funds for Rhode Island College. He found an enthusiastic supporter in Moses Lindo, who had studied at the Merchant Taylor's School in London, but as a Jew, had not been officially registered or granted a diploma. Moses Lindo was a rare type of individual in colonial America. He was a technologist. His specialty was the processing of indigo dye from the plant of that name, which was grown in South Carolina and was, next to rice, the colony's largest item of export. Lindo had arrived in Charlestown on *The Charming Nancy* in 1756 as a representative of a group of London textile manufacturers who used great quantities of the royal blue dye. As an expert on indigo, or "indico," Moses Lindo did the selecting, appraising, and shipping. Later he was appointed by the governor "Surveyor and Inspector General of Indigo," an honorary title, since the only money he made was the commissions he received from the indigo planters.

The indigo expert had studied chemistry and he experimented with other vegetable dyes. One of them was a crimson dye which he extracted from a South Carolina berry. He wrote an article about it which was published in *The Philosophical Transactions* of the Royal Society in 1763. Moses Lindo died in 1764, shortly before the Revolution put an end to trade with Great Britain and ruined his beloved indigo industry. His modest estate was sold "at public outcry" in a back store on the Bay, where most of Charlestown's business was conducted.

8. *The Jews in the American Revolution*

At the time of the American Revolution there were about 2,500 Jews in the American colonies, though some sources put their number as high as 3,000, others as low as 1,500. The total population of the 13 colonies was about two and a half million. The Jews were a tiny minority, but a significant one. Their significance lay in the very fact that they were a minority. The words of the Declaration of Independence, "All men are created equal," held out a hope of freedom and equality to every group and individual, regardless of his creed or national origin. The Jews, who had been driven from so many places, and denied every human and legal right, saw in the successful outcome of the Revolution their chance to participate as free citizens in the building of a new nation. The Jewish minority was historically important as well. It was the nucleus of one of the largest and most varied immigrant groups to come to America in the nineteenth and twentieth centuries.

Jews took part in the revolutionary struggle from the start. We have seen how the Jewish merchants, who were engaged in shipping and overseas trade, protested vigorously against the Navigation Acts and the Stamp Act. When fighting broke out, they continued to give support to the American cause. Early in the war the British captured Newport and the Jews of Newport chose to leave their homes and places of business rather than collaborate with the British. In general, the Jews were no different from other colonists, some of whom remained loyal to King George, while most joined the ranks of the revolutionists. Philadelphia became the gathering place for American patriots, and to Philadelphia came Jews from Newport, New York, Charlestown, and Savannah, Georgia. Americans liked to compare their struggle against tyranny to the ancient struggles of the Israelites. The Liberty Bell, which was cast 25 years before the Revolution, bears an inscription from the Old Testament, "Proclaim liberty throughout all the land unto all the inhabitants thereof" (Leviticus 25:10).

In their fight against Great Britain the colonists received help from France, partly because France was herself at war with England, but also because the ferment of the French Revolution was already at work. General Lafayette came from France to help the colonies, and the Polish generals, Kosciuszko and Pulaski, exiles from their own country, also fought in the Revolution. Jews from Europe were drawn into the fight as well. Benjamin Nones, born in Bordeaux, France, came to Philadelphia in 1777 and enlisted in Captain Verdier's regiment under General Pulaski. He fought in all the battles of the Carolinas and at the siege of Savannah. He became a colonel at the head of 400 men, many of whom were Jews. At the battle of Camden, South Carolina, General de Kalb, a professional soldier who had come with Lafayette, was critically wounded and it is said that Nones helped carry him from the field of battle. After the war Benjamin Nones went to Philadelphia where he became an official interpreter of French and Spanish for the new government. Nones was an ardent supporter of Thomas Jefferson and when he was attacked in the newspapers he replied, "I am a Jew . . . and for that reason am I a republican. In republics we have rights, in monarchies we live but to experience wrongs."

Francis Salvador owned an indigo plantation in the northwestern part of South Carolina. He came from London in 1773 and soon became associated with other Carolina planters and was elected to the Provincial Congress from his district. He has the distinction to have been the first Jew elected to a popular assembly, because this provincial congress became the first Assembly of the State of South Carolina after independence was declared. When the British fleet attacked Charlestown he joined the state militia and became an officer. His regiment had to defend "the back country" which was being overrun by Tories and hostile Indian tribes. On August 1, 1776, his regiment was ambushed by the Indians. He was shot down from his horse and then scalped. He died so early in the Revolution that his name appears only in South Carolina history. A plaque dedicated to his memory in Charleston reads:

> Born an aristocrat, he became a democrat,
> An Englishman, he cast his lot with America;
> True to his ancient faith, he gave his life
> For new hopes of human liberty and understanding.

Mordecai Sheftall was a native of Savannah, Georgia. He was a prosperous merchant and according to the British, "a very great rebel." He became chairman of the Rebel Committee of Christ Church Parish (Savannah) and Commissary General of Purchases and Issues. It was his task to purchase food and supplies for the fighting forces and he was so meticulous in the discharge of his duties that he left

Robert Morris, George Washington, and **Haym Salomon** stand in Heald Square, Chicago. *(Courtesy Chicago Historical Society)*

numerous letters, accounts, and receipts behind, which are a good source for the student of the day-to-day events of the war in the South. When Savannah fell, he was captured by the British, put on a prison ship with his son, and taken to the West Indies. He underwent quizzing by the British, and suffered many humiliations both as a Jew and a rebel. After the war he received a grant of land from the American government in recognition of his services.

There is a monument in Chicago (erected in 1941) which has three figures — George Washington in the center, on one side Robert Morris, and on the other Haym Salomon. Robert Morris was the Superintendent of Finance during the Revolution. Since Congress had no power to impose taxes, raising money to pay, feed, and clothe the army was a formidable task. Loans came from France and Spain, but these were in the form of notes which had to be cashed or "discounted." Haym Salomon was the broker who discounted these notes. More than that, he made personal loans to Jefferson, Randolph, Madison, and other delegates to the Continental Congress. James Madison, who was to become the fourth President of the United States, wrote to his friend Edmund Randolph that he was resorting to loans from Salomon, "with great mortification," because "he obstinately rejects all recompense...To a necessitous delegate he gratuitously spares a supply out of his private stock."

Who was Haym Salomon? He was born in Lissa (Leszno), Poland, left home as a boy, traveled all over Europe, learned many languages, and acquired a thorough knowledge of banking and finance. After the partition of Poland in 1772 he went to London, and two years later came to New York. He became associated with American patriots, was arrested by the British as a spy and condemned to death. Somehow he escaped and went to Philadelphia where he advertised himself as a broker and then offered his services to Robert Morris. He was a practical man who helped the American cause in practical ways. That he did it generously without much gain to himself shows that he was also an idealist. He donated a large sum of money to the building of the Philadelphia synagogue in 1782, and later sent money through Amsterdam business agents to his needy parents in Poland. Though he had handled huge sums for the American government, at his death he left very little to his family.

At the end of the Revolution each of the 13 states had its own constitution and its own set of laws. Some states had outlawed slavery. Some had religious restrictions on voting and holding office. These were enforced in indirect ways. For instance, before accepting office, a person had to swear a Christian oath, which a Jew couldn't do. Thomas Jefferson, then governor of Virginia, opposed such restrictions. In 1786 the state of Virginia, under Jefferson's influence, passed the Statute of Religious Liberty, which gave equal civil rights to people of all religions. Soon the other states followed Virginia's example. By the time the new nation was established it was the only nation in the world which granted the Jews economic, religious, and political equality with other citizens.

PART II

The Jews from Germany and Central Europe: 1820-1880

1. *Medieval Myth*

In 1820 Sir Walter Scott, the English poet and novelist, published *Ivanhoe*, a romantic novel about the Crusades, set in twelfth century England. One of the heroines in *Ivanhoe* was the beautiful and spirited Rebecca, daughter of Isaac, the Jew, a miser who was torn between love for his daughter and his money. Scott modeled his heroine after Rebecca Gratz about whom he had heard from his American friend, Washington Irving. Irving, the author of "The Legend of Sleepy Hollow" and "Rip Van Winkle," had met Rebecca Gratz at the home of his fiancée in Philadelphia. Born in 1781, the daughter of the well-to-do merchant, Michael Gratz, she was a charming and cultivated young woman who moved in the best social circles. In later life she became devoted to good works and founded a home for orphans and the first Hebrew Sunday School Society in 1838. It seems odd that Sir Walter Scott had to go so far afield to find a model for the exotic Rebecca over whom knights fought in tournaments. In describing her and her miserly father he was, in fact, following a literary convention which was founded on myth.

Until well into the nineteenth century few Christians in Europe mingled with Jews on an equal footing. There had been Jewish communities in medieval Europe, not only in Spain, but in Italy, France, the Rhineland, and Bohemia. But the Jews were excluded from feudal society. They were neither lords nor vassals—they could not own land or work on it. They were considered the king's chattels and he could do with them as he pleased. If he found them useful, they stayed; if not, he expelled them. Some Jews found places at Court as the king's personal physicians, more often as moneylenders and treasurers who provided the money the king needed to fight his wars. In return the

Rebecca Gratz (1781-1869) of Philadelphia.
Sir Walter Scott drew upon Washington Irving's
description of Rebecca when he wrote *Ivanhoe*,
published in 1820.

king gave the Jew his protection, sometimes his friendship. A king or
a feudal baron might boast of his clever and resourceful "Court Jew"
as he might boast of his court jester or troubador.

Jews who lived in towns and were craftsmen, such as goldsmiths,
weavers, tailors, or shoemakers, were not admitted to the Christian
guilds. If they were merchants they had to pay heavy taxes for the
privilege of doing trade. Indeed, they had to pay taxes simply for
permission to live in the town. They were not allowed burghers' rights,
couldn't hold office or mingle freely with the other townspeople. But
as long as they could work they managed to get along and sometimes
to prosper.

Susskind von Trimberg (right), a German
troubadour of the thirteenth century. His
conical hat marked him a Jew.

On the continent and in England the feudal vassals, who were tied to the land and oppressed by the nobles, looked upon the Jews with hatred and suspicion. The Jews seemed to have more freedom than they. They were learned — they knew how to read and write and often spoke more than one language. Above all, they knew the language of numbers. They could do sums and handle coins with ease. Besides, the Jews practiced a different religion from their neighbors, followed strange customs, observed their own holidays, ate different foods. Weird tales began to be circulated about these mysterious people. They were devils in disguise, they had tails like monkeys, hidden under their long gaberdines, they used Christian children's blood in their rites, they practiced witchcraft. The clergy and nobles found it to their advantage to encourage these tales. If a peasant lost his bit of land, if the crop failed, or a child died of the plague, someone had to be blamed. It was easy to lay the blame on the Jew. And so a myth grew up of the diabolical, miserly Jew who owned treasures that everyone coveted. One of his treasures was gold; the other a beautiful daughter. Two hundred years before Sir Walter Scott wrote *Ivanhoe*, Shakespeare had drawn on this myth when he created the beautiful Jessica and her miserly father, Shylock, in *The Merchant of Venice*.

2. *The Ghetto*

There were not many Jews in England until modern times. They had come from France with William the Conqueror in 1066, were expelled in 1290, and not allowed to return until Oliver Cromwell gave them permission to do so in 1656. For two centuries Jewish life in England followed a pattern like that of medieval Europe. The Plantagenet kings borrowed money from them to fight the barons. A wealthy Jew, Aaron of Lincoln, even loaned money for the building of abbeys and of Lincoln Cathedral.

Lending money at interest was denounced by the Church as usury, and so this despised calling was shifted onto the Jews, even though the Jewish religion also forbade usury. The law required that the money-lenders accept "pledges" from the borrowers. When the borrowers couldn't redeem these pledges the Jews were accused of avarice and greed. They accumulated some wealth in the form of armor, jewels, houses, even costly church plate. But the kings and barons generally managed to get it back in the form of taxes, or simply by seizing it. In time even money-lending was forbidden to the Jews and they became wretchedly poor. They crowded into the towns in special quarters assigned to them and followed humble occupations. Threadneedle Street in London, on which a handsome synagogue once stood, gives a clue to one occupation they followed.

Nearly every city in Europe had its Jewish quarter. In Imperial Rome it had been called by a Latin name—*Vicus Judaeorum.* In Spain it became *Judaria,* in France *Juiverie,* in Germany *Judengasse,* in Austria and Bohemia *Judenstadt.* Often these quarters grew up naturally near a Hebrew academy, a busy marketplace, or a synagogue. Living close together the Jews felt safer from outside attack.

In the sixteenth century these Jewish quarters became known as ghettos. No one is sure about the origin of the word *ghetto,* but the most commonly held theory is that it came from the word *giotto,* a cannon foundry near which the Jewish quarter in Venice was located. It was about this time that the ghettos lost their voluntary character and became compulsory. In 1556 Pope Paul IV established the first compulsory ghetto in Rome on the left bank of the Tiber. The Roman ghetto was enclosed by a high wall and had a gate which was locked from sundown to sunrise, as well as on Sundays and Christian holidays. The Jews were not allowed to live anywhere else in the city. It became a model for such ghettos in the rest of Europe.

The rules varied from place to place. The Jews were made to wear a yellow badge, a peaked hat, a long gaberdine, or some other distinctive garment. In Rome they had to march in a procession once a year carrying their *Torahs,* or Scrolls, and beg permission of the Pope to allow them to remain another year. In most places they paid a heavy tax. If they were allowed to trade outside the ghetto walls, this trade was hedged in by various rules. For instance, they might sell used clothing (but not new garments), old jewelry, and second-hand goods of all kinds. This gave the Jewish merchants a shabby, transient character and turned most of them into old clothes and junk dealers. Going through the marketplace with their yellow badges, carrying their stock of goods in and out of the ghetto wall, they were often jeered and insulted by the populace.

The ghetto in Frankfurt, Germany, early nineteenth century.

Because certain areas were designated for the ghettos they soon became overcrowded. New stories had to be added on top of old houses. The streets were narrow and gloomy, often dirty. Little sunlight and air penetrated the densely built up areas. When the compulsory ghettos were finally abolished, the term *ghetto* continued to be applied to any poor and crowded neighborhood occupied by Jews, and later by other segregated minority groups.

Life in the European ghettos was not always mean and squalid. In Frankfurt-am-Main, Trieste, and Prague the ghettos were cities-within-cities. Mayer Amschel Rothschild (1743-1812), the founder of the Rothschild banking family, had an impressive house in the Frankfurt ghetto. The Prague ghetto was famous for its Talmudic academies to which Hebrew scholars flocked from all over Europe. The Jews of Prague had an autonomous government, with a chief rabbi, a council of elders, and their own courts of law. They had their own town hall, and four craft guilds, of goldsmiths, tailors, butchers, and shoemakers. Holidays were celebrated with pageantry. There were feasts and processions, and once a year a kind of carnival called *Purimspiel* during which troupes of players put on masks and costumes and enacted the *Spiel* or play about Queen Esther and Haman. At one time the religious leaders in the ghetto became alarmed at all the display and began exhorting their people to pay less attention to feasting and fine clothing, and more to prayers and acts of piety, just as the prophets of old had exhorted the people of Palestine.

In medieval France, bands of armed men attacked the Jews in their homes and synagogues. The massacres were often led by Crusaders on their way to chase the Turks out of the Holy Land.

Even while the ghettos were becoming a way of life for the Jews of western Europe, certain forces began driving them out. The Crusades were one such force. Armed bands who gathered to march against the Saracens in the Holy Land first turned on the "infidels" at home. With the cry of "Death to the Christ-killers!" fanatical mobs roamed the cities, looted and burned Jewish homes and synagogues, tortured and killed those who tried to defend themselves. Rather than give up their faith or submit to torture, thousands of Jews chose to die by their own hand. Mothers killed their children, then leaped into the Rhine and drowned. Young men tried to resist and died. Elderly men marched in processions carrying their sacred scrolls and chanting *"Shema Isroel,"* "Hear Oh Israel," as they went to their death.

Another force was the Black Death, or Plague, which ravaged Europe in the twelfth and thirteenth centuries. In their ignorance of what caused the Plague, the people blamed the Jews for casting evil spells and poisoning the wells and rivers. They believed that if the Jews were driven out, the Plague would go. Driven from western Europe and Germany by the Crusades and the Black Death, and by wars such as the Hussite War in Bohemia, the Jews began to look about for new places of refuge.

3. *Poland*

To the east of Germany in wide, fertile fields and plains, and among deep forests lived a Slavic people who had been pagans until they came under the influence of the Roman Church in the tenth century. Between the tenth and thirteenth centuries, they accepted

Christianity, fought off several Tatar invasions, and formed the kingdom of Poland. Poland was an agricultural country made up of large estates owned by nobles, or *pans*, and cultivated by peasants. A middle class was needed to build up the towns and develop trade with the West. For this purpose the Polish kings began to import German traders and craftsmen. In 1264 King Boleslav invited the Jews from Germany to settle in Poland. As an inducement he issued a charter which gave the Jews freedom to travel, offered protection from attack, and declared the slanders against them to be false. More Jews came to Poland when Casimir the Great (1330-1370) gave them the right to buy or rent land anywhere in the kingdom.

Poland extended its boundaries to Lithuania and the provinces on the Baltic Sea, as well as to Galicia and the Ukraine on the Rumanian border. Under the benign rule of the Polish kings Jews settled in every corner of the land, and established in the towns and villages communities called *kahals*. These kahals built schools and synagogues, and set up courts of law and societies for the care of the sick and poor. The Jewish craftsmen organized their own guilds. Jews leased and administered salt mines, became agents and overseers on the estates of the *pans*, and collected taxes from the peasants.

The Ukraine had once belonged to the Cossacks, a proud and warlike people, who had more in common with the Tatars than with the Poles. They resented the rule of the Polish nobles and clergy. Poland was Roman Catholic, and the Cossacks were of the Greek Orthodox faith. Their church was taxed, and the tax collector was often a Jew, who had the keys to the church and wouldn't open it until the tax was paid. Oppressed by the Polish nobility, the Cossacks came to hate and resent their agents, the Jews.

This resentment flared up in the Cossack uprising of 1648. Led by their Hetman (headman) Bogdan Chmielnicki, who had been trained in wars against Turkey, the Cossack horsemen overran the Ukraine and the nearby provinces of Podolia and Volhynia. In rebellion against the Poles, they also vented their hatred against the Jews. They stormed into synagogues, slashed the holy arks, trampled on the scrolls, and set fire to the wooden structures. They mutilated, tortured, and killed the inhabitants of whole villages.

When **Bogdan Chmielnicki** (1595-1657) led the Cossacks of the Ukraine in an uprising against Polish rule, his men killed thousands of Jews. Chmielnicki put the Ukraine under Russian protection in 1654. Ten years after his death Russia and Poland divided the Ukraine between them.

The Cossacks rode west and besieged Lwow (Lemberg), demanding that the city council surrender the Jews. When the town council refused, they asked for a ransom and after collecting the ransom, killed the Jews anyway. The Cossack wars lasted off and on for seven years. During that time between 300,000 and 400,000 Jews died, were driven out, or were sold into slavery to the Turks. The Chmielnicki massacres have been called the greatest disasters the Jews suffered until the time of Hitler.

One of the towns of the Ukraine that lay in the path of the Cossacks was Pereyeslav, which 200 years later became the birthplace of the Jewish writer, Sholom Aleichem. Sholom Aleichem wrote with humor and sympathy of the people who lived in the little towns and hamlets of the Ukraine. In a story called "The Town of the Little People," he described a town which he called Kasrilevka and spoke of its old cemetery, rich in graves, which "They [the Jews] still value as they might a treasure, a rare gem, a piece of wealth.... For this is...the place where their ancestors lie, rabbis, men of piety, learned ones, scholars and famous people, including the dead from the ancient massacres of Chmielnicki's time..." Two hundred years after the event these "massacres of Chmielnicki's time" had become part of folk legend.

The Jews of Poland who survived the Cossack massacres never regained the privileges they had enjoyed under the early Polish kings. Poland itself became involved in foreign wars and in civil strife and lost much of its territory and prestige in Europe. Outbreaks against the Jews became common. Frightened and bewildered by the hostility of the people around them, the Jews shrank more and more from contact with the outside world. As often happens with a persecuted people, they fell prey to strange superstitions, began to believe in omens and evil spirits, and welcomed many self-appointed "messiahs" and miracle workers.

Early in the eighteenth century a man appeared who called himself Baal Shem Tov — Master of the Good Name. He founded a movement called Hasidism, which emphasized joy rather than gloom, kind deeds rather than formal piety. It did some good by revitalizing religious beliefs and making the hard lot of the people more bearable, but it set its adherents even farther apart from the outside world. By "outside world" we mean western Europe toward which some Jews were beginning to return.

4. *Return to the West — Fall of the Ghettos*

The Chmielnicki uprisings in Poland coincided in western Europe with the end of the Thirty Years' War (1648). This had been mainly a religious war and when it was over, both Catholic and Protestant countries turned to rebuilding their ruined economies. With the passing of the feudal system, the religious persecutions of the Middle Ages had disappeared. The people in general became less superstitious and bigoted in their outlook. The emphasis on economic development and the rational spirit of the age favored the Jews. The descendants of those who had once fled eastward began to return to western Europe.

Holland which had received the Sephardic Jews earlier in the century now began to admit Ashkenazim from eastern Germany and Poland. Amsterdam became famous for its Jewish scholars, philosophers, and scientists, for its shipping merchants and craftsmen in gold and silver and precious stones. The Dutch masters used Biblical subjects in their paintings as well as scenes from contemporary Jewish life and portraits of notable Jews.

A group of Amsterdam merchants petitioned Oliver Cromwell, the Lord Protector of England, to lift the ban on the Jews. He complied not only for humanitarian but for practical reasons. The Jewish directors of the East India Company had international contacts and he needed their services. We have noted earlier that some of the Sephardic Jews of England came to settle in America.

Portrait of a Rabbi by Rembrandt van Rijn (1606-1669). Rembrandt lived for many years in the Jewish quarter of Amsterdam. Among the Jews he found models for some of his finest portraits as well as for drawings and etchings of Biblical subjects.

Germany was still divided into a number of states. Frederick the Great of Prussia (1712-1786) singled out certain Jews for favor and gave them special privileges such as the right to travel and to live in certain cities, like Berlin. These "favored" Jews helped to make Germany a great industrial nation by building textile factories, railroads, and later electric plants. Many distinguished themselves by their scholarship. Moses Mendelssohn, who had been born of a poor family in Dessau, came to Berlin and became the founder of the Jewish movement called the *Haskalah* or Enlightenment. He translated the five books of Moses into German with a parallel text in Hebrew. From this text of the Bible the Jews learned the German language.

Most of the German Jews still lived in ghettos. In the border province of Alsace-Lorraine they worked as peddlers and moneylenders. Strasbourg, the capital of Alsace, admitted these peddlers only during the day. In the evening a loud blast from a trumpet drove them back to their ghetto-slums in outlying villages. Other towns in the Rhineland imposed on the Jews special taxes and limited their places of residence and occupations.

At the same time during the eighteenth century, philosophers in England and France were spreading the new doctrine of the rights of man. There were oppressed people everywhere, peasants and townspeople without legal rights, often without work. Economically these people were even worse off than the Jews. These were the people who answered the call of the French Revolution, stormed the Bastille, and overthrew the French monarchy. It was the French Revolution and the events that followed it which finally overthrew the Jewish ghettos.

In 1791 the French Assembly granted equal rights to the Jews of France. After the French Revolution Napoleon was hailed as a liberator by many small countries and minority groups which had been under German or Austrian rule. His troops marched into the Rhineland and Italy, and wherever French soldiers marched in, they battered down the walls of the ghettos. As the ancient walls crumbled, martial bands played, fireworks were set off, and people cheered and embraced each other—both Jews and their Christian neighbors.

The breaking down of the ghetto walls had a double result. It brought thousands of Jews, especially in France, into contact with the outside world, and gave them a chance to enter trades and professions. At the same time it did away with some of their old privileges of autonomy and self-rule. The Jews were now guided not by their rabbis and elders, but by the law of the land. For instance, one of the rights granted by the French Assembly was the right to civil marriage. French Jews became Frenchmen first, and Jews only in respect to their religion. Later this happened in Germany as well. The German Jews considered themselves to be Germans "of Hebraic or Mosaic persuasion."

Synagogue of the Portuguese Jews in Amsterdam, dedicated in 1674.

The *Judengasse* or Jewish quarter
of Vienna. Late nineteenth century.

5. *The Jews from Germany*

Between 1820 and 1870 the population of the United States increased from 10 million to 40 million. Most of this growth was due to the great waves of immigration from central Europe, and especially from Germany. Because the census listed the immigrants by the country they came from, such as Germany, Austria, or Bohemia, it is hard to determine just how many of the immigrants were Jews. In 1820 there were roughly between 4,000 and 5,000 Jews in America. It is estimated that by 1850 there were between 40,000 and 50,000 and that by 1880 there were almost 10 times that many. What were the reasons for this large immigration?

The chief reason was economic necessity. The population of Europe had grown tremendously in the early nineteenth century, and the Jewish population, in spite of wars and massacres, and in some places bans on Jewish marriages, had grown even more in proportion to the general population. The Industrial Revolution, which had started in England and spread to the continent, favored only the rich entrepreneurs, both Christians and Jews. Thousands of peasants left their farms and villages and crowded into the cities to work in mills and factories. Others had gone to America. Very often the innkeepers, shopkeepers, and craftsmen in the villages had been Jews. When the countryside emptied, they were left without a source of livelihood. There was no place for them in the cities. The only solution was to emigrate. In doing this they had a precedent. Many adventurous young men from Jewish families had left their homes to seek their fortunes in the New World. Ocean travel was becoming more common, and thousands of Jews from Germany, from western Poland, from Austria and Bohemia gathered in the Atlantic seaports — Bremen, Hamburg, Le Havre — and waited for ships to take them across the ocean.

Immigration societies were formed in Berlin, Vienna, and Prague to help the poorer immigrants. They traveled steerage, herded together among cattle and pigs, sleeping on wooden shelves arranged in tiers, eating food that was "hardly fit for cattle back in Bohemia," as one of the immigrants wrote in his diary. But the voyage lasted only a few weeks — after that came America, and the horizon was the limit.

The horizon lay to the west. Native Americans were crossing the mountains in covered wagons, staking out land in the western territories. The homesteads they left behind were taken over by German peasants, many of whom settled in Pennsylvania. German Jews settled among them, as they had in the old country. Others followed the wagon trails. They lacked the skills we usually attribute to pioneers. Since they hadn't been permitted to work on the land in Europe, they didn't know how to fell trees, plow the earth, or plant crops. Roadbuilding, mining, and what we call heavy industry had little attraction for them. It was difficult work with little recompense or chance for advancement. But the German-Jewish immigrants didn't lack an adventurous spirit. Distance didn't daunt them. They were willing to travel far, on foot if necessary, to endure hardships, to face loneliness. Most of the German Jews started out as peddlers, with a basket or pack on their back, filled with useful gadgets, cutlery, "notions" such as combs, scissors, needles, thread — anything and everything that the pioneer men and women might need. Yankee peddlers had preceded them. Farm women living far from towns were accustomed to dealing with itinerant vendors and welcomed their coming. Quite often they were European immigrants themselves and were glad to have a chance to talk to a peddler in their native language.

Some peddlers were more clever or perhaps luckier than others. They made enough money to buy a horse and buggy and a bigger stock of wares — perhaps farm implements, carpentry tools, pots and pans and dress materials for the women. If they came to a town or village that looked prosperous they opened a general store, a hardware store, or dry goods business. In a few years they saved up enough money to send for their wives and children, for brothers and sisters. They wrote letters to Frankfurt, to Strasbourg or Posen, urging friends to join them in the new land. Others, who were not so lucky, went on peddling on foot or sank to the level of hoboes and tramps. Their families back home perhaps never heard from them again.

The middle western cities were chosen by many German Jews. Cincinnati, Ohio, dates its first Jewish community from 1824, Louisville, Kentucky, from 1832, Chicago, Illinois, from 1837. Germans and German Jews came to Milwaukee and other cities in Wisconsin. Jewish immigrants followed the gold rush to California. In 1849, the year of the gold rush, a Yom Kippur service was held in a tent in San Francisco. In western mining towns Jewish merchants sold supplies to gold and silver prospectors. The heavy denim pants called levis were first manufactured by a Jewish peddler named Levi Strauss in California.

In 1848 revolutions broke out in nearly every country in Europe. The failure of the revolutions set off a new wave of immigration. Many of the German Jews who came to this country after 1848 were intellectuals—teachers, writers, musicians—who did much to enrich the cultural life of America. Their struggle against European monarchy made them value American democracy and wish to preserve it. They joined the abolitionist movement and fought in the Union armies during the Civil War.

Rabbi Isaac Mayer Wise (1819-1900), leader of Reform Judaism in the United States. Born in Bohemia and educated in Vienna, he came to America in 1846. Wise led a congregation in Cincinnati for 46 years, and worked to unify the Reform congregations in America.

Rabbi David Einhorn (1809-1879), born in Bavaria, came to Baltimore in 1855. He spoke out against slavery, and thus tangled with Rabbi Wise on that issue as well as on points of doctrine. Threatened by a proslavery mob, he left Baltimore in 1861. Einhorn later led Reform congregations in Philadelphia and New York.

But not all Jews were on the side of the North. Some who lived in the South favored the Confederacy. Judah P. Benjamin served under Jefferson Davis as Secretary of War and Secretary of State. Rabbi Isaac Mayer Wise of Cincinnati, a leader of the Reform Synagogue movement, sided with the South, and there were rabbis who quoted the Bible in their sermons to prove that slavery was divinely ordained. In opposition to them Rabbi David Einhorn of Baltimore preached in favor of abolition. On the subject of slavery and states' rights the Jews were as divided among themselves as the rest of the American people. Politically as well as economically the Jews had by the time of the Civil War been absorbed into the mainstream of American life. This was a far cry from the old European ghettos where the Jews had had no status as citizens at all, and could not voice their opinions on any matter that concerned the country they lived in.

The nineteenth century was an era when most of the great American fortunes were made. It was still possible to go "from rags to riches" in one generation, to start like Andrew Carnegie as a bobbin boy, and end as a steel magnate. Some of the fortunes, mainly in retail business and to a smaller extent in manufacturing and banking, were made by Jewish immigrants from Germany who had started out as pack peddlers.

Nathan Straus (1848-1931) and his brother Isidor were partners in the R. H. Macy Company. During the panic of 1893, Nathan opened milk stations and lodging houses for the poor. He also led a 20-year campaign for the pasteurization of milk. His brother **Oscar Solomon Straus** (1850-1926) was a lawyer, diplomat, and cabinet member.

One of these men was Lazarus Straus, who came from Bavaria in 1852, and traveled through Georgia first with a peddler's pack, then with a horse and buggy. Then he opened a shop in Talbotton, Georgia, and sent for his wife and three small sons. After the Civil War, Lazarus Straus and his three sons, Isidor, Nathan, and Oscar, left Georgia and moved to New York where they opened a crockery business. In 1871 the Straus brothers rented a corner in the basement of Macy's department store for a china and glassware display. By 1888 they had become partners in the R. H. Macy Company and with imaginative merchandising skill turned it into a huge department store, which became the model for others. The Straus brothers were noted for their many civic and philanthropic activities. Oscar Straus was envoy to Turkey and Secretary of the Department of Commerce and Labor under President Theodore Roosevelt. A member of the third generation, Jesse Isidor Straus, became Ambassador to France. Adam Gimbel and Benjamin Altman also started as peddlers and became owners of large New York department stores.

Baiersdorf, Germany, was the birthplace of the seven Seligman brothers who began their business careers as peddlers in Alabama. Joseph Seligman was the first to come to America, in 1838, and his brothers followed him. Jesse lived in Selma, Alabama, and Joseph had a drygoods store in Greensboro. In 1862 they moved to New York and started a banking firm, which formed branches in New Orleans,

The banking firm of **Joseph Seligman** (1819-1880) provided financial aid to the Union during the Civil War. **Solomon R. Guggenheim** (1861-1949), one of Meyer Guggenheim's seven sons, founded a museum of nonobjective art in 1937. His fine collection of twentieth-century paintings was moved to Frank Lloyd Wright's structure on Fifth Avenue in 1959.

San Francisco, Frankfurt, London, and Paris. Joseph Seligman was a good friend of General Ulysses Grant and a staunch supporter of President Lincoln. His firm obtained loans in Europe for the United States Government and after the war continued to give financial support to the U.S. Navy. In a manner characteristic of the German Jews Joseph Seligman was the founder of such organizations as the Hebrew Orphan Home and an Ethical Culture Society. He was a member of the Board of Education in New York and president of the American Geographical Society.

Perhaps the most spectacular of the family fortunes was the one made by the Guggenheim brothers, of whom there were also seven. Their father, Meyer Guggenheim, came from a small town in Switzerland where his family had lived for 200 years. In 1847, Meyer, who was then 19, began to peddle merchandise with a horse and buggy in the coal mining towns of Pennsylvania. Later he manufactured lye and stove polish and sold imported Swiss embroideries. In the 1880's he invested in some silver and lead mines in Colorado, then in copper mines and smelters. It was in copper that the Guggenheim fortune was made.

His sons expanded the industry and became patrons of art, music, and the sciences. One of them endowed the Guggenheim fellowships. Another founded the Guggenheim Museum in New York to house his collection of modern paintings and sculpture.

6. *Religious and Community Life*

In the European ghetto the synagogue was not only a place for worship, but a house of study as well. The body of accumulated knowledge was large. It contained not only religious doctrines and the history of the Jewish people, but rules governing everyday conduct, philosophical discussions, parables, folk tales, legends, and poetry. A child could begin by learning the Hebrew alphabet, go on to reading the Bible, and continue to study and discuss the more difficult books such as the Mishna and Talmud all through his life. Prayers were an everyday obligation, which could be performed either in the synagogue or at home. The rabbi did not necessarily lead in worship. Rather he was a leader of the community, a teacher and a judge. He would interpret the law and pass judgment on any question — from a divorce case or business dispute to a minute point of dietary law, such as whether a pot in which milk had been boiled could be used for cooking meat. He was also responsible for the community's welfare. Though the ghetto Jews paid taxes to the state, they got almost no benefits in return. They were responsible for their own charities. Indeed, their religion laid this obligation upon them. The Hebrew word *zedaka* for charity or benevolence, also means justice. To provide for the poor, the sick, and the aged was simply an act of justice.

In America this pattern could not be duplicated, nor was it desirable. It had already begun to vanish in western Europe after the fall of the ghettos. The Jews adapted themselves to the laws and

Benjamin Altman (1840-1913). In 1906 he built his second department store at Fifth Avenue and 34th Street. B. Altman & Co. was so popular that it drew the rest of the New York shopping center uptown with it. Altman left his large collection of paintings to the Metropolitan Museum of Art.

Hebrew Union College in Cincinnati, Ohio. Founded in 1875 by Rabbi Isaac M. Wise, it is the oldest rabbinical school in the United States.

customs of whatever country they lived in. In America this process of adaptation came about naturally. When we speak of a "Jewish community" in an American city we use the term in a loose sense. It was only a community insofar as its members felt they shared certain traditions, customs, and religious observances, and wished to preserve them.

We have seen how the early Jewish settlers bought burial plots so their dead could be buried in consecrated ground. They continued to do this in the nineteenth century. In the large cities there was more than one Jewish cemetery. As immigration increased each group that came tended to form its own little enclave. This was especially true of the synagogues. By the time of the Civil War there were between 50 and 60 synagogues in New York alone, representing German, Polish, Spanish, Dutch, Russian, English, and Bohemian Jews. Sometimes the members of one European community or of one trade formed their own congregation. If they couldn't afford a building, they rented a vacant store or a basement in a tenement house.

The rapid growth of houses of worship extended to social life. Since there was no central authority, no chief rabbi or council as there had been in the past in Europe, the immigrants formed numerous mutual benefit societies or *chevras*. Some were quite small and perhaps had only one function, such as visiting the sick, or providing an insurance or loan fund for its members. Others enlarged their scope and became social clubs as well, providing entertainment and often cultural activities such as literary discussion groups, choral societies, and orchestras. The young men's Hebrew literary societies of the nineteenth century gave rise much later to the Y.M.H.A.'s patterned somewhat on the Y.M.C.A.'s. There were also many fraternal orders established, similar to the Masons. Such an organization was the Independent Order of B'nai B'rith founded in 1843, with lodges in many cities. By 1860 it had a membership of 50,000.

In the 1850's and 1860's the German Jews began building hospitals in the larger cities. One reason for these hospitals was that Jewish patients who observed the dietary laws couldn't get kosher food in the general hospitals or those run by Christian denominations. Jewish orphanages and homes for the aged began to appear at that time. The history of Jewish charitable and welfare organizations is so complicated that we can only make a note of it here.

Education had been a matter of concern for the early settlers. The first synagogues tried to maintain schools for children, but Jewish parochial education never became widespread. In the 1840's when the compulsory public school system came into existence, Jewish children began to attend public schools, and the old synagogue schools dwindled and finally disappeared. In the 1860's the last barrier to public school education was overcome when schools no longer required attendance on Saturday, the Jewish Sabbath. For religious instruction Jewish children went to Sabbath or Sunday schools which were conducted in English, or to afternoon Hebrew schools which taught the Hebrew language, as well as religion. Both types of schools have always been voluntary.

The first synagogues in America followed the Sephardic ritual. This was an Orthodox ritual. In 1824 a group of 47 members of *Beth Elohim* congregation in Charleston, South Carolina, led by Isaac Harby, tried to institute some reforms in the ritual. They wanted to shorten the service, introduce English into the prayerbook, and have the rabbi give a sermon in English. When the trustees refused this request, they seceded and formed their own congregation. Eight years later they returned, but by that time "reform" was in the air.

The Jews arriving from Germany had been influenced by the Reform movement which had started in Hamburg and Berlin. One of the innovations of that movement was the introduction of organ music. This was a hotly debated question, since the Orthodox synagogues had allowed only choral music. In the Orthodox synagogue women sat in a separate section from the men, usually in the balcony. The men wore some sort of head covering, and a prayer shawl. No part of the service was in the vernacular language, and there was no "sermon" in the modern sense of the word. The proponents of Reform argued that to many worshipers the Hebrew prayers were meaningless and that the whole ritual was antiquated.

In their zeal to modernize the ritual they threw a great deal of it overboard. The Reformed temples, as they were often called, were in many ways closer to some Protestant churches than to the old synagogues. So much so, that the East European Jews often recoiled from them in horror. This was not the "old-time religion" as they knew it. The classic façades of the temples fronted by pillars, the stained glass windows, choir lofts, organs, the sermon in English seemed alien to them. They continued to worship in their accustomed fashion, or to make compromises between the old and the new. Out of the conflicts of the nineteenth century there emerged the three large divisions of organized Jewish religion—Reformed, Conservative, and Orthodox. Each of them has changed with the changing times. The Reformed temples have re-introduced some of the old customs and the others have modernized some of theirs.

PART III

The Jews from Eastern Europe: 1880-1924

1. *Russia and the Jewish Pale of Settlement*

In the latter part of the nineteenth century, when immigrants began pouring into this country at an unprecedented rate, the largest single group, next to the Italians, were the Jews from Eastern Europe. They came from a scattered area—thousands, for instance, came from Rumania and the Austrian province of Galicia, but by far the largest number came from Russia, or to be more exact, from the Jewish Pale of Settlement in the Russian empire.

What was this Pale of Settlement? Historically it was not very old— it had only existed since the latter part of the eighteenth century. In earlier times few Jews had lived in Russia proper. Only rarely were Jewish merchants from Poland and Germany allowed temporary entry to the great Russian trading fairs. Even Peter the Great (1682-1725), who imported German, Dutch, and English shipbuilders, stonemasons, mechanics, and merchants to help him westernize his backward country, excluded the Jews. During the eighteenth century era of enlightenment in the West, Russia was still a feudal country with an autocratic Czar, a powerful Greek Orthodox Church, a small landed nobility, and millions of serfs attached to the land. At the close of that century, when the American people had declared their independence from Great Britain, and the French people overthrew the Bourbon monarchy, Catherine the Great of Russia expanded her empire by annexing most of Poland. In the Ukraine, the Baltic countries, and Poland lived one million Jews. At practically one stroke they became Russian subjects. What was to be done with them? The Czarina, Catherine, solved the problem by defining a boundary beyond which they might not go. This border area into which the Jews were confined became known as the Jewish Pale of Settlement.

Catherine the Great (1729-1796) became Czarina of Russia in 1762. Under Catherine, Russia expanded westward, taking over the rest of the Ukraine and most of Poland. On December 21, 1791, Catherine established the Jewish Pale of Settlement.

The Czars who followed Catherine the Great—Alexander I, Nicholas I, and Alexander II—kept shifting their policies in respect to the Jews. At times the Pale was enlarged, then it was restricted again. A decree would go out that the Jews leave the rural areas and move into the towns. Then the decree was revoked. Jews were allowed to have homes in some towns, others required special permits. A permit might be good for only 24 hours, and if a man was caught out of bounds, he had to pay a fine. Russian officials were open to bribes, and the Jews learned to live with a corrupt government.

At one time the Jews had their own self-governing bodies or *kahals*. These kahals were now stripped of all their powers except that of collecting taxes. And the taxes imposed on the Jews were twice as high as those for other groups. The government policy toward education kept shifting also. Nicholas I had a minister who argued that the only way to absorb the Jews was to educate them. For this purpose "crown" schools were established. At first the Jews welcomed them, but it soon became apparent that the main function of these schools was not to educate but to make converts. A decree went out that the Jews select rabbis to conduct government business—issue birth certificates, perform marriages, officiate at funerals, settle legal disputes. These were called "crown rabbis," and since they were puppets of the government, they were extremely unpopular with the people. Whenever they could, the Jews tried to avoid the decrees,

The Jewish Pale of Settlement in the late nineteenth century included 15 provinces of western Russia, as well as Russian Poland. The rest of Russia was closed to Jews, except for doctors and certain merchants who were allowed to live in some cities of the interior. The Pale was officially abolished during the Russian Revolution of March 1917.

some of which, if properly carried out, might have been to their ultimate advantage. Instead of availing themselves of "crown" benefits, they stubbornly maintained their own schools, went to their own rabbis for advice and the settling of disputes, and organized their own welfare societies.

The law that was hardest to evade was the compulsory military service. In Russia during the first half of the nineteenth century men had to serve in the army for 25 years. A cruel law by any standards, it had an additional feature in the case of the Jews, which made it barbaric. Jewish boys were conscripted at the age of 12 instead of 18, and had to spend six years in a "cantonment" in order to be indoctrinated into the Greek Orthodox faith before they began their 25 years of military service. Parents whose sons were taken into service mourned them as dead. Even if a man survived the brutal life of the army camps and didn't die on the battlefield, he came out after 31 years a complete stranger to his own people. Nobody sent his child willingly. Since every town or village had to produce a certain number of recruits, gangs of *chappers* (kidnapers) roamed the countryside and literally snatched children away. If a rumor came that a gang of kidnapers had been seen, parents hid their boys in the woods or even had them crippled or maimed. This law was so difficult to carry out that eventually the Russian government had to modify it. In 1855 during the reign of Alexander II, the 25-year term of service was changed to six years and the "cantonment" was done away with. It seemed to the Jews that a new and better day was dawning. When in 1861 Czar Alexander II freed the serfs all of Russia rejoiced, including the Jews, of whom there were almost three million now. They felt that the new Czar was truly a liberator.

This was not entirely the case. When 47 million serfs were set free, their masters were compensated for their loss, but the serfs themselves were not given any land. They only swelled the great mass of landless, impoverished Russian *muzhiks* (peasants) who lived in squalid huts together with the pigs and cattle. They could neither read nor write, and believed anything the village priest chose to tell them.

Alexander II and his advisers, like the German rulers a century before, were astute enough to see that the Jews could be useful. The domicile laws were relaxed in some cases to allow the wealthier Jews and those who qualified as skilled mechanics to establish residence in Moscow and a few other cities in Russia proper. The "crown" schools were abandoned and a certain number of Jewish students were allowed to enter the regular gymnazia (high schools) and universities. A Jewish professional class came into existence—doctors, lawyers, teachers, engineers. Some went abroad to study and came back from

Alexander II (1818-1881) became Czar of Russia in 1855. He freed the serfs in 1861 and undertook partial reforms of the courts, the army, and local government. Problems of land distribution caused discontent and led to Alexander's assassination by a terrorist in 1881.

Rural villagers of the Ukraine.

England or Germany with liberal ideas. In 1863 a Polish rebellion, in which Jews also took part, was crushed. Political "criminals" were exiled to Siberia. Others left the country. But the mass of the Jewish people was not affected. Political rebellion at that time was a luxury for the educated and comparatively well-to-do. Most of the Jews simply wanted to be left alone. These were the millions who lived packed together as tightly as "herring in a barrel" throughout the towns and villages of the Pale of Settlement.

2. *Village Life*

The typical Jewish village or small town of the Russian Pale differed from the sixteenth century ghetto of western Europe. It was not enclosed like a fortress by a stone wall. Rather it was set off from the rest of the world by an invisible barrier made up of folk customs, religious observance, and a close-knit community and family life. Most of the people were poor. They worked as cobblers, tailors, carpenters, glaziers, draymen. A few kept taverns or small shops. A man who had neither a trade nor a shop might travel about the countryside with a horse and wagon or even on foot to see what he could find for a small bit of money. He might pick up a rusty plow which he could clean, or a piece of lumber, and exchange it with a peasant for a bag of grain, or other produce to take to the market. He seldom traveled so far that he couldn't get back to his family before the Sabbath.

The Sabbath began on Friday after sundown. No matter how poor a family was, even if it lived on potatoes and cabbage all week, some coins were set aside to buy fish or meat and a white loaf for the Friday evening and Sabbath dinner. The men hurried to the synagogue for evening prayer. The children had been bathed and dressed in their best clothes. The women, who had scrubbed and cooked during the day, now lit the Friday night candles. Up and down the narrow streets from every window these candles glimmered. The good smell of food cooking filled the house. There was a saying that a person could starve any day of the week, but nobody had ever starved on the Sabbath. Even the town's paupers and tramps, who slept on synagogue benches and lived on handouts, were assured of one hot meal during the week. For it was a duty, even an honor, to share the Sabbath meal with a guest. If a stranger arrived in town or was stranded during a journey (traveling was forbidden on the Sabbath) he went to the synagogue knowing that someone would offer him hospitality.

Families were large, with three generations often living under one roof. Marriages were arranged by the parents of young people, often with the help of a professional matchmaker. Perhaps the father

A carriage-maker (left) and a cobbler, both of Warsaw.

A *cheder,* or elementary Hebrew school. The *melamed's* elderly father is seated at the left.

returned from a journey with good news; "*Mazel tov* (congratulations), Rachel," he said to his daughter, "you're engaged to be married." Rachel didn't dare ask to whom. Very often the betrothed couple didn't see each other before the wedding. "Time enough to get acquainted later," the old people said in jest, which was tinged with sadness. They knew that life would be hard. There was hardly such a thing as a carefree time of youth. In Jewish law divorce was allowed, but it was not very common. The birth of a child was a happy occasion and small children were tenderly cared for. But school began early, at the age of five, sometimes sooner. Boys were sent to *cheder* (elementary Hebrew school) where they studied from early morning until dark with little free time for play. The *melamed* (teacher) was often underpaid and burdened with cares of his own, and he was expected to exercise authority. He dealt out slaps and cuffs indiscriminately.

Though the countryside was not far away, Jewish children seldom went swimming or fishing or roaming in the woods. Some of the holidays, however, brought nature to them. During the fall holiday *Sukkoth,* every family built its own little *sukkah* or hut and decorated it with branches and autumn fruits. *Lag b'omer,* a holiday in early summer, was similar to Arbor Day. The winter holidays had their own kind of merrymaking and were a welcome release from school.

We see from this that piety and learning were held in highest regard; they were more important than wealth. It was not at all rare for a man to devote his whole life to study and prayer. A young man who devoted himself to studying the Torah and Talmud might have a father or father-in-law who supported him and his family. Often his wife earned the family living. There were many capable and energetic women, who not only managed their households and raised their children, but operated a business of some kind, perhaps a tavern or shop. Women were not given a voice in community affairs and they sat apart from the men in the synagogue, but they were respected and honored in the family circle. This was during a time when a Russian peasant's wife was considered her husband's property and wife-beating was not only common but sanctioned by law. The Jews differed in other ways from their peasant neighbors. Drunkenness, the peasant's way of finding release from a life of toil, was rare among the Jews. So were crimes of violence, such as murder. Life in every form was held sacred.

These traits which characterized the Jews of the Pale of Settlement — a willingness to work hard and subsist on little, loyalty to family ties, regard for learning, rigid piety, and a moral obligation toward life — they brought with them to the New World.

A grandfather teaches his small grandson to read.

Gesia Street in the Jewish quarter of Warsaw. After the pogroms of the 1880's many Russian Jews settled in Warsaw. By the eve of World War II Warsaw had a Jewish community of 370,000 — the largest in Europe.

3. *The Immigrants*

Alexander II was assassinated in 1881, and his successor, Alexander III, took stern measures to crush any hint of rebellion. The various nationality groups within the Russian Empire — Polish, Latvian, German — were forbidden the use of their native languages in the schools. Strict censorship was imposed on books and newspapers. Loyalty to "Mother Russia" became the watchword, and Mother Russia was synonymous with the Czar's government. The Jews bore the brunt of the attack. The Russian peasants were incited by village priests and officials, and bloody massacres, or *pogroms,* broke out all over the Pale of Settlement. After the turn of the century armed gangs called "The Black Hundreds" marched against the Jewish villages with religious banners, portraits of the Czar, and the cry of "Down with the Jews!"

In May 1882 the Czar issued a set of Temporary Rules, which became known as the "May Laws" and which threw the life of the Pale into chaos. These laws were complicated, but in general they were intended to break up the Jewish villages and small towns and force the inhabitants to move into larger towns, which were already intolerably congested. For example, Jews were not allowed to settle "anew" in another village, even if they had inherited property in it or wanted to join their families. Local authorities were given the right to expel any Jews they didn't want and to seize their homes. In some places the Jews had been allowed to work at a craft but not to engage in business. This rule was now interpreted to mean that a man could produce something, but not sell it. Thousands lost their means of livelihood. The schools and universities lowered their quotas so that it was almost impossible for a Jew to enter a Russian school. Jewish lawyers were not admitted to the bar, and doctors were hedged in by restrictions.

Alexander III (1845-1894) became Czar of Russia after his father's assassination in 1881. His repressive measures set off a mass emigration of Jews from Russia.

In 1891 when the Grand Duke Sergei became Governor of Moscow he gave an order that all the Jews leave the city at once. Between 15,000 and 20,000 Jews of Moscow were rounded up and escorted out of town under police guard. Where would all these displaced and unemployed people go? As the Czar's minister, Pobedonetsev, cynically remarked, one third would die, one third would leave the country, and the rest would become absorbed into the general population, that is, lose their identity as Jews.

At least one part of his prediction came true. Hundreds of thousands of destitute and desperate people began leaving the country. They were granted exit permits, but since these required long waits and bureaucratic red tape, many crossed the borders secretly at night. They streamed into the border towns of Germany and Austria. The Jews of these countries became dismayed at the masses of refugees, hungry, ragged, and often ill from exposure, who looked to them for assistance. The German Jews at first tried to stem the tide, to plead with these people to go back. They sent delegations to the Czar to intercede on their behalf. When fresh pogroms broke out, such as the

A rare photograph of a group of young revolutionaries gathered before the body of a friend killed in the Kishinev pogrom of 1903.

Kishinev pogrom of 1903, heads of foreign governments, including President Theodore Roosevelt, sent notes of protest to the Czar. The protests were ignored. The Jews of western Europe began helping the refugees. The *Alliance Israelite Universelle*, which had been formed a few decades before to help victims of cholera epidemics, now sent committees to the border towns to help the refugees with money, clothing, and medical care.

The Russian Jews scattered over western Europe and England. Since ocean travel had improved and steerage accommodations were less primitive than they had been, many emigrated overseas to South America, South Africa, and Canada. But for most of them the ultimate goal was the United States of America. About two-thirds of the ocean liners which carried immigrants docked in New York harbor.

Before entering New York the immigrants had to undergo an examination at Ellis Island. Congress was trying to keep out undesirables and there was always the danger of being sent back. To people weary from the long journey and afraid of anything "official" this was a terrifying ordeal. There were organizations to help them, notably

Three students who were active in self-defense measures during the Kishinev pogrom, 1905. Morris Lerner (left) later emigrated to South Dakota where he established a farm under the Homestead Act. Ben and Nathan Gelfand became grocers in Minneapolis.

HIAS (Hebrew Immigrant Aid Society) which sometimes provided interpreters. The language they had to interpret was usually Yiddish.

If he passed the physical examination and answered successfully a long list of questions, the immigrant's passport was stamped and he was ready to leave Ellis Island for the Barge Office at the tip of Manhattan Island.

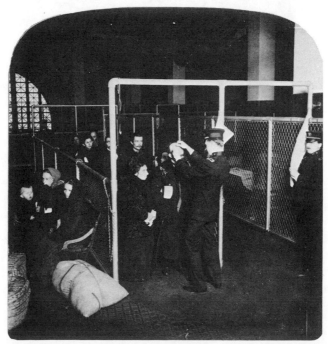

Inspectors examine the eyes of immigrants. Ellis Island, 1913.

4. New York's East Side — People at Work

The saying was, "In America people rake up gold in the streets."
The immigrants didn't believe this as a literal fact, but even as a
symbol it was no longer true. The limitless horizon was gone. The
frontier had been settled; the great fortunes had been made. By the
1880's America was becoming increasingly urban, and the new Jewish
immigrants, instead of setting out for the road with a peddler's pack,
congregated in the large cities — New York, Philadelphia, Boston,
Chicago. A few had the dream of "going back to the land," and joined
cooperative farming communities, in South Dakota, Oregon, the
Middle West. With the exception of some in New Jersey these didn't
last long.

Sabbath eve in a cellar. Photograph by Jacob A. Riis, 1890.

A newcomer wandering around New York, frightened and dazzled
by the tall buildings and bustling crowds, deafened by the roar of the
elevated train, might run by chance into a landsman (townsman) from
the old country, who told him about opportunities in St. Paul, Minnesota, or Atlanta, Georgia, where life moved at a slower tempo.
He listened and risked his few dollars on a train ticket. More often
than not he remained in New York.

Pushcart peddler. In 1898 an estimated 1,500 peddlers sold their wares on the Lower East Side. Each cart had a specialty — clothing or crockery, fruit or pickles, boots or fish.

The reasons for staying in New York were simple. A man with little money and a family to support had to find work and a place to stay right away. In proportion to their number there were more women and children among the Jewish immigrants than among other groups. Before laws were passed to prohibit contract labor, groups of men had come from the Slavic countries to work on railroads and in mines. The Jews didn't do this. They brought their families and came to stay. On the East Side of New York they found work as cigar-makers, garment workers, and pushcart peddlers. A dignified old man with a beard and a skullcap who had sat over the Torah in his native town might be seen selling pretzels on Hester or Rivington Street. Another man sat bent over a sewing machine 17 hours a day, or stood at a pressing board pushing a heavy steam iron back and forth. Young girls worked in crowded factories which were draughty in winter and stifling in summer, and a health and fire hazard at all times. Men earned between six and ten dollars a week, women and girls between four and five dollars. This type of work was called "the sweatshop system."

It was not really a system at all, since it had grown up in a haphazard fashion. Earlier in the century clothing had been custom-tailored or sewed at home. The invention of heavy sewing machines and steam presses, and the increased demand for ready-to-wear clothing had given rise to the garment industry. Since the manufacture of clothing required less outlay of capital than heavy industry, it had attracted

"I cash clothes." Many immigrants were too old to learn a new trade or too poor to set up a shop. They supported themselves by buying and selling old clothes.

the earlier Jewish immigrants from Germany, who by the latter part of the century owned most of the garment factories. The owners, instead of carrying out the whole manufacturing process, divided it up with contractors. The factory-owners employed skilled cutters who cut out the garments on their premises, then sent the bundles of cuttings to the contractors, who in turn hired workers to do the basting, sewing, pressing, and finishing. The contractors rented a loft in a rickety building, or used their own tenement flats as shops, crowding machines and workers into every available corner. If the workers complained they were told to leave. There were plenty of fresh immigrants coming off the ships every day to take their place. The contractors were not necessarily cruel and inhuman. They were themselves the victims of a wasteful and chaotic method of production.

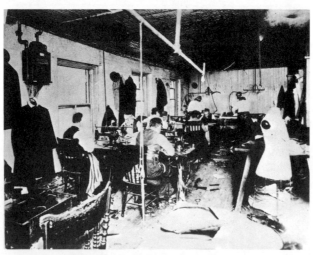

Sweatshop, 1910. A garment was usually made by a team of three: the machine operator, the baster, and the finisher.

Moe Levy & Co. Clothing Factory, about 1912. The factory system was faster than the shop system. Each worker made only one part of the garment, over and over again.

Every now and then something happened that brought to the notice of the public the appalling conditions of the sweatshops. On March 25, 1911, a fire broke out at the Triangle Waist Company, which employed girl workers. Several girls jumped to their death from a seventh floor loft and 146 died in the fire. Later the states began enacting safety legislation, but meanwhile the workers themselves had begun to organize unions which eventually reduced the work week to 40 hours, raised the wages, and improved working conditions.

The labor movement had been growing all over the country. In 1881 several craft unions joined together under the leadership of Samuel Gompers, a Jewish cigar-maker from London, into an association which gave rise to the American Federation of Labor. The "needle trades," as the garment trades were sometimes called, went through a long trial-and-error period until they formed the two giant trade unions. The workers in men's clothing formed the Amalgamated Clothing Workers of America, in 1914, with Sidney Hillman as president. He held this post until his death in 1946. In the 1930's Hillman became one of the founders of the CIO (Congress of Industrial Organizations) and he was one of President Roosevelt's advisers during the New Deal.

The other great union, the International Ladies' Garment Workers (ILGWU), was founded in 1900 and took part in 1910 in a strike which lasted two months, involved 60,000 workers, and resulted in a history-making settlement, called "The Protocol of Peace." The man who negotiated this settlement was Louis D. Brandeis, then a Boston lawyer, who was later to become a Justice of the Supreme Court. This settlement provided for an Arbitration Board, Grievance Committees and other innovations which later became standard practice in labor-management relations.

The two great garment workers unions, the Amalgamated, under Sidney Hillman, and the ILGWU under David Dubinsky, pioneered in other matters concerning labor. They had a system of unemployment insurance before the Federal government took over that function. They also started a program of auxiliary service for the workers. They built cooperative, low cost apartments, established health centers, nurseries, and summer camps, as well as adult education classes, and lecture and concert series. *Pins and Needles,* with book by Marc Blitzstein and songs by Harold Rome and others, was put on with a cast made up entirely of garment workers of the ILGWU in 1937. It had songs of social protest in the style of the thirties, such as "Sing Me a Song of Social Significance," and after Chamberlain's Munich pact, "Britannia Waives the Rules," as well as catchy boy-meets-girl love songs. Planned originally as a week-end entertainment for union members, it made stage history by becoming the most successful musical to that date and played on Broadway for three years.

The greatest accomplishment of the unions, of course, was that they abolished the sweatshop system. In recent years, the membership, which had been made up of East European Jewish immigrants, was in large part replaced by Italians, Negroes, and Puerto Ricans. But the leaders of the garment unions have often been Jews who had started as workers in the shops.

Sidney Hillman (1887-1946), president of the Amalgamated Clothing Workers from 1914 until his death. He came from Lithuania in 1907. **David Dubinsky** (right) became president of the ILGWU in 1932. A Pole, he came to America in 1911 after escaping from a Siberian prison.

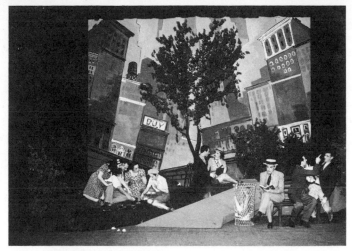

Sunday in the Park—a scene from *Pins and Needles*, staged by garment workers in 1937.

5. *The People's Speech*

Hebrew, the language of ancient Palestine and of modern Israel, was for the immigrants the language of the Bible, the Talmud, and the book of prayer. Their everyday speech was Yiddish. Hebrew and Yiddish have the same alphabet, and on the printed and written page they look almost alike. But the spoken languages are quite different from each other.

As the Jews moved about from place to place, they learned the language of each country. The Sephardim, besides speaking Spanish, used among themselves a language that was a mixture of Spanish and Hebrew and was written in Hebrew characters. This was called Ladino. In the Middle Ages in Germany the Jews began speaking the local dialect—Middle High German. Again, they mixed Hebrew words with it, and wrote it in Hebrew. This was the language they brought with them to Eastern Europe. Since the German word for Jew, *Jude*, became *Yid* in Eastern Europe, the language was called *Yiddish*. In Poland and Russia the language acquired many Slavic words, but it remained basically Germanic.

For many centuries in Europe the Yiddish language was not held in high esteem. It was called "jargon," literally gibberish. Scholars and serious writers wrote their books in Hebrew, just as medieval scholars had written in Latin, scorning the vernacular languages of their day. But a vernacular, or everyday language, becomes stronger

and richer with use. That is what happened to Yiddish. At first it was considered only suitable for doggerel verses, light romances, and folk tales. It became a literary language when in the latter part of the nineteenth century writers began using it for lyric poetry, plays, stories, and novels. Its former drawbacks became its virtues. Since it was a mixture to begin with, it was flexible and easily incorporated new words and phrases. Because it had been used by ordinary people— laborers, draymen, peddlers, and vagabonds—it had a strong, earthy quality. What it lacked in grammatical complexity, it made up in a varied vocabulary. Though it had been lightly dismissed as "women's language" and "kitchen talk," it was not trivial. Women did more than exchange gossip. They sang lullabies to their children. Grand- mothers talked about the old days in the little towns, about flights and pogroms, about sons who had been impressed into the army or had run off to America. And so the language had a strain of tenderness and melancholy. It also had wit, and a wry kind of humor. The Jews, who had survived so many upheavals and disasters, had learned to turn a phrase into a joke upon themselves.

As the immigrants began learning English, they mingled English words and phrases with their Yiddish. The children and grandchildren, born in America, spoke English almost exclusively. But as the use of the Yiddish language declined, a strange thing began to happen. Yid- dish words and phrases cropped up on the stage, in novels, and more recently on radio and in television. Some became current usage and have been included in American language dictionaries. A recent magazine article has this title: "Around the World with Thumb and Chutzpah." We all know what "thumb" means to a traveler. *Chutzpah,* a Yiddish word of Hebrew origin, meaning insolence or impudence, has been mellowed by usage to mean a jolly kind of daring or nerve.

6. *The Yiddish Press*

In an era when newspapers were numerous and highly competitive the Yiddish language press was no exception. It has been estimated that at one time there were 12 Yiddish papers published in New York alone, and that their combined circulation was over half a million. It was the largest and most diversified of any foreign language press. Yiddish weeklies and monthlies had been started in the 1870's, but the first daily paper, the *Tageblatt* (Jewish Daily News), came out in 1885 and lasted 43 years before it merged with other papers. It was believed to be the first Yiddish daily in the world. The Yiddish papers reflected every shade of political opinion, from the conservative and religion-oriented *Tageblatt* and *Morning Journal* to the Zionist *Day*, the socialist *Forward* (est. 1897), the communist *Freiheit* (1922) and smaller philosophical-anarchist papers. These papers carried on a constant rivalry among themselves, not only in print but in arguments among the editors, writers, and intellectuals who gathered in the East Side cafés to drink tea and discuss the issues of the day.

The Jewish Daily Forward, September 15, 1897. In the cartoon Czar Nicholas II, surrounded by bodies, tries to strike a bargain with Uncle Sam.

Though printed in Yiddish, the only language their public knew, the papers were far from parochial or narrow. Their aim was to educate the new immigrants and to help them become Americanized. Besides national and international news, they printed articles on American government and history, instructions on how to become naturalized citizens, news about unions, clubs, and fraternal organizations, and articles on popular science. Every paper printed letters from readers asking for advice on domestic problems. Of these the *Forward's Bintel Brief* (Bundle of Letters) became the best known. The Yiddish dailies and weeklies devoted more space to literature than American papers. They printed translations of European and American classics, and novels by Yiddish writers in daily installments. Among the working people in the ghetto there were many self-taught poets and writers who contributed poems, short stories, and essays dealing with the everyday lives of the immigrants. There were also well-educated journalists who produced book reviews and drama criticism of a high caliber.

Among the Yiddish journalists Abraham Cahan (1860-1951) stands out. He had graduated from a teachers' institute in Vilno, Lithuania, and taught elementary school for a short time, until his participation in revolutionary activity made it difficult for him to remain in Russia. He came to New York in 1882, and worked at various odd jobs — as a cigarmaker, a teacher, editor of a small weekly paper — until in 1897 he helped found *The Jewish Daily Forward.* He left this paper to work for an American newspaper, *The Commercial Advertiser,* but returned in 1902 as editor and built up the *Forward* into a great newspaper with a circulation of 200,000 at its peak. Cahan was deeply concerned about the problems of the sweatshop workers and he did a great deal, both as an editor and a speaker, to help the unions which were at that time trying to get a foothold. Politically, the *Forward* was a socialist paper with moderate leanings.

The *Commercial Advertiser,* on which Cahan worked for several years, was a lively, crusading New York paper edited by Lincoln Steffens, who later became known as a "muckraking" reformer and wrote books exposing corruption and graft in big city politics. At the *Advertiser* Abraham Cahan met and became friendly with a young writer, Hutchins Hapgood, who had been born in Illinois, but was of old New England stock and had graduated from Harvard. When Hapgood was given an assignment to write a series of sketches about the Jewish immigrants of the East Side, it was Cahan who acted as his guide and interpreter. Cahan introduced him to old Hebrew scholars, fiery young Russian radicals, workingmen and shop girls, artists and actors and writers. Hutchins Hapgood's sketches were published in book form in 1902 and reprinted in 1967, under the title *Spirit of the Ghetto*. Hapgood was lucky in finding just the right illustrator, a young Jewish artist named Jacob Epstein, who sketched portraits of East Side characters. He lived and worked in the garret of a tenement overlooking Hester Street, in the heart of the ghetto. Jacob Epstein later moved to England, where he became a renowned sculptor, and was knighted.

Cahan wrote and published stories and novels in English. In 1917 he published *The Rise of David Levinsky*, which has become a classic of Jewish immigrant life. It is possible that the title was suggested to him by the title of an earlier American classic, *The Rise of Silas Lapham*, by William Dean Howells, which came out in 1885. *Silas Lapham* dealt with the conflict between an enterprising Yankee

Going to the Synagogue. A charcoal drawing by Jacob Epstein from Hutchins Hapgood's *The Spirit of the Ghetto*, 1902.

businessman and old Boston aristocracy. Howells, the editor of the *Atlantic Monthly* and *Harper's* for many years, knew Cahan and encouraged him in his writing. By helping each other, and collaborating when the opportunity arose, these writers and artists were weaving a new strand into the texture of American life.

7. *The Yiddish Theatre*

The East Side Jew's favorite form of entertainment was the theatre. The pool halls, saloons, and hangouts of the Bowery—the poor man's usual places of amusement—had little attraction for him. This doesn't mean that the theatre was necessarily of a serious or uplifting nature. On the contrary. The early Yiddish theatre consisted of melodramas interspersed with vaudeville acts, light operas based on Biblical and historical subjects, sentimental sketches, and broad farce. Later, under the influence of serious playwrights and of such actors as Jacob Adler and Maurice Schwartz, a realistic element was added in "slice-of-life" plays which presented the true life of the ghetto. But whatever the play was—tragedy or comedy or farce—the audience participated with gusto. They laughed, cried, hissed, cheered, and applauded the actors. On weekend nights whole families turned out, including children and babies in arms. During intermissions they bought souvenirs and refreshments, talked with old friends and met new ones. In its popular appeal the Yiddish theatre was not unlike the Elizabethan theatre of Shakespeare's day.

The history of the Yiddish theatre has been traced to the synagogue ritual. The Talmud forbade theatre as a form of "idol worship," but the Jews had always loved music, especially vocal music. In the synagogue the service was conducted by a cantor, who sang or chanted the prayer, with emphatic intonations, while the congregation made a rhythmic response. Some European cantors had developed a highly individual style, and people came a great distance to hear them. Such a cantor was young Zelig (later Sigmund) Mogalesco, the cantor at the Bucharest synagogue. He had been a child prodigy, had traveled through Rumania and southern Russia, and had led a choir of 20 men at the age of 14.

Grand Street Theatre, about 1900.

In 1876 a man named Abraham Goldfaden heard him sing and decided that the young cantor had not only a remarkable voice but a talent for acting. Goldfaden was a Russian Jew with a talent for writing and singing. After he had failed in business, he became a sort of music-hall performer; he wrote poems, set the words to popular tunes, and sang in Rumanian taverns. Goldfaden wrote a play and persuaded young Mogalesco, who was then 20, and several members of the synagogue choir to make up the cast. The play was an immediate success, and the troupe began touring various towns in Rumania and Russia. Since women were not allowed on the stage, Mogalesco often played women's parts with great success. He developed a talent for comedy. In a few years Goldfaden had enlarged his repertory and was hiring women as well as men.

In 1883 the Russian government outlawed the Yiddish theatre on the pretext that it was a hotbed of political intrigue. Immigration to America had already started and Goldfaden's troupe went to New York, where a ready-made audience awaited them. He hired a theatre which he called the Rumania. Other acting groups arrived from Europe and soon there was the Germania, the People's, the Windsor, the Thalia, and others, playing to full houses on the Bowery. Forgetting the old Talmudic injunction against "idol worship," the theatre lovers almost worshipped their favorite actors. One of the matinee idols of the day was Boris Thomashefsky, a dark, handsome, rather heavy-set man with curly black hair and a simpering manner who played romantic leads. The European-bred audiences preferred their stars, both male and female, to be on the plump side, in the style of early opera singers.

Jacob P. Adler (1855-1926), father of a theatrical family, toured Russia with Goldfaden's troupe and came to America in 1887. One of his greatest roles was in the Jewish *King Lear*. (Right) sheet music from *Lear*.

To satisfy the growing demand several playwrights turned out plays by the hundred, often borrowing from novels and other plays. Shakespeare was popular on the Yiddish stage, both in straight translation and in adaptations. There was a Yiddish version of *Hamlet* and *Othello* and a Jewish *King Lear*. Ibsen's *The Doll's House* had its counterpart in a play called *Minna* in which the heroine did more than slam the door on her loutish husband. She committed suicide by drinking carbolic acid. *God, Man and the Devil* was adapted from Goethe's *Faust*. After the turn of the century Jewish playwrights were producing original plays based on Jewish life and folklore. In the 1920's there were 12 Yiddish theatres in New York and several in other large cities, as well as numerous touring companies. They produced a number of excellent actors, some of whom later distinguished themselves in the American theatre.

Paul Muni (1895-1967), born in Austria, made his stage debut in Cleveland at the age of 12 in a Yiddish skit called *Two Corpses at Breakfast*. He joined Maurice Schwartz's Jewish Art Theatre in 1918, and in 1928 he went to Hollywood. A great character actor, Muni won an Oscar for *The Life of Louis Pasteur*.

Herschel Bernardi traveled the Yiddish theatre circuit with his parents and spoke his first onstage lines at the age of three. Among his television roles was that of Lt. Jacobi in *Peter Gunn*. Bernardi played Tevye for two years in the Broadway production of *Fiddler on the Roof*.

8. *Food*

What are knishes? Kreplach? Kneidlach? You will find them all under the letter K in the index of a Jewish cookbook, or you can order them in a Jewish restaurant. In some places knishes are sold like hot dogs or pizza and eaten out of hand. They are a kind of baked pastry filled with chopped meat, mashed potato, or a mixture of both. Kreplach are triangle-shaped pockets of noodle dough usually filled with chopped meat (though there are cheese kreplach too) and served like noodles or dumplings in soup. Kneidlach are dumplings of various types; the best known are the matzo balls served in chicken soup.

The above trio, like most Jewish foods, are derived from Central or East European sources. Sometimes you can guess the origin of a dish by its name. Blintzes are thin pancakes filled with cottage cheese, and folded like little plump pillows, then fried in butter and served with sour cream. They are related to Russian blini. Borscht, a soup made of beets and served cold, with sour cream, is a variant of one of the many kinds of Russian *Borshch* or Polish *Barshch*. Hot cabbage borscht, made with meat stock and containing a number of other vegetables, is none other than the hearty cabbage soup of the Russian peasant. Buckwheat kasha (*kasha* means cereal) and buckwheat pancakes come from Eastern Europe where buckwheat was cultivated. Rumanian *mamaliga*, on the other hand, resembles American cornmeal mush. Indian maize, or corn, was imported to Rumania from America and became a staple of that country's diet. Another dish from Rumania is an appetizer made of eggplant, which has been first broiled over a flame to give it a characteristic smoky flavor.

Yonah Shimmel's Knishery on Houston Street in New York City. Established in 1910, the knishery is now run by the founder's grandson.

Strudel, a rich pastry which is served at every Jewish wedding and celebration, is of Austrian origin. Making the paper-thin "stretch dough" for strudel is a culinary art developed by Viennese pastry cooks. Cheese cake, honey cake, and kichel (cookies) come from Central or Eastern Europe. So do pumpernickel and rye bread, with or without caraway seeds. Nobody knows who invented the bagel, that doughnut-shaped hard roll which gets its special texture from the fact that it is boiled before being baked. In this country bagel-and-lox has become a popular combination. Lox is smoked salmon. All kinds of fish — salted, pickled, and smoked — appear in Jewish delicatessens. The word delicatessen itself is German, though it comes from the French word, *delicatesse.*

Jewish delicatessens sell kosher corned beef, pastrami (spiced beef), salami, and other prepared meats. In Jewish neighborhoods there are also butcher shops with the word *kosher* on their signs. This means that the meats have been prepared according to *kashruth,* the Jewish dietary code. This code which comes from a Mosaic law forbids the eating of pork, which is called *treif* — meaning forbidden. All other domestic animals and poultry are eaten, but they have to be slaughtered in a prescribed way by a man trained for this job, who is called a *shochet.* Some parts of cattle, like the hind legs, are not eaten, but liver and tongue are kosher. Shellfish, incidentally, are not kosher. In addition, an old Biblical injunction not to "seethe a kid in its mother's milk" was construed to mean that milk or milk products, such as cheese and butter, should not be eaten with meat.

Limited as they were by these rules, Jewish cooks had to use considerable ingenuity in preparing their food. Since many of them had to be frugal as well, they used the materials that were cheap and plentiful, such as dried beans, peas, lentils, root vegetables, and dried fruits. A dish made of meat with carrots, or meat with potatoes and prunes, is called a *tsimess*. Cooks experimented with this dish by adding various ingredients and flavorings, and the word *tsimess* became part of a slang phrase. When someone wanted to say, "Don't exaggerate," or "Don't make a mountain out of a molehill," he said, "Don't make a whole tsimess out of it."

The Jewish holidays all have their special foods. Passover celebrates the escape from Egyptian bondage. Since the fleeing Israelites had no time to wait for their bread to rise, they ate flat cakes of unleavened bread. This is the *matzo* which is eaten instead of bread during the days of Passover. At the *seder* or Passover supper, a plate with symbolic foods is placed on the table. It contains horseradish to symbolize the bitter days of bondage, *charoseth*, a mixture of chopped apples, nuts, and wine, for the mortar which went toward the building of the pyramids, a bone of the Paschal lamb, and a sprig of parsley or other green vegetable to denote hope and the coming of spring.

Purim celebrates the feast of Queen Esther and the downfall of Haman, the enemy of the Jews. Cookies filled with prunes or poppyseed and shaped like triangles to represent Haman's hat are called *hamantashen*. And on Friday night, which ushers in the Sabbath, there is the large braided loaf of white bread, the *challah*, a bottle of wine, and that other traditional dish, gefilte fish, a type of fishball, usually accompanied by red or white horseradish.

The seder table, Passover.

75

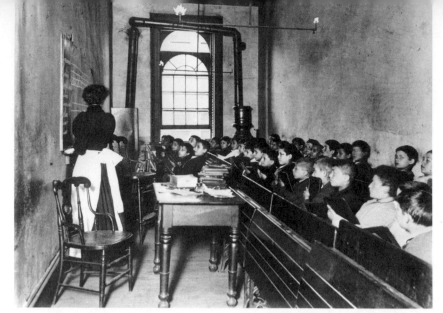

A class in the condemned Essex Market School, New York City. Photograph by Jacob A. Riis, about 1890.

PART IV

The American Experience: Twentieth Century

1. *Transition*

We have seen how the Jews in early America and those who came in the nineteenth century from Central Europe and Germany had adapted themselves to the American environment. Their descendants, feeling their own position to be secure, looked upon the masses of East European Jews pouring into the country with apprehension mingled with pity. The words inscribed on the pedestal of the Statue of Liberty applied to all immigrants, but they had been originally inspired by the plight of the East European Jews. America had indeed opened her "golden door," but would she be able to absorb these "huddled masses yearning to breathe free/The wretched refuse of your teeming shore"?

In the large cities welfare organizations formed by Jews of German descent and settlement houses built in slum areas worked hard to "Americanize" and "civilize" the immigrants. Often welfare workers making their rounds found to their surprise that the people they were trying to civilize had a rich and meaningful culture of their own and were quick to adopt American culture as well.

This was especially true of the children of immigrants. When a family arrived from Europe, the older children often had to work to help support the family, while the younger children went to public school. Both at work and in school the children learned the new language and new customs fast. Too fast, it seemed to their parents. They played in the street with other children (often of Italian or Irish descent), picked up American slang, adopted a whole new folklore, incomprehensible to their parents. In Hebrew school the children had been taught to admire the heroes of Jewish history — the Maccabees and Bar Kochba. Now they had a whole new set of heroes — prizefighters and baseball players. In the synagogue they chanted the sacred music; in the street they picked up the tunes of Tin Pan Alley and American jazz. It could hardly be otherwise, for in the early years of the century what we now call "popular" American culture had its beginnings. To this popular culture many Jews made a significant contribution.

Playing under a street sprinkler. New York City, 1915.

Irving Berlin wrote his first song, "Marie from Sunny Italy," when he was a singing waiter in Chinatown. Berlin has composed for films as well as for the stage. *Top Hat, Holiday Inn,* and *Easter Parade* include some of his most familiar songs.

In 1911 "Alexander's Ragtime Band" was all the rage. It had been written and composed by Irving Berlin, who was born in Russia in 1888 and came to New York with his family as a small child. His father was a part-time cantor in a synagogue, his olders brothers worked in sweatshops and sold newspapers. At the age of nine after his father's death, Irving Berlin left home and earned his keep by leading a blind singer around the saloons on the Bowery. Later he became a singing waiter (like Eddie Cantor) and began composing songs for musical revues and plays, among them *Annie Get Your Gun* and *Call Me Madam.*

Education had always been important to the Jews, both for its own sake and as a means of advancement. As the economic lot of the immigrants improved, their children stayed in school longer, and went on to high school and college. Even before World War I the sons and daughters of East European Jews were beginning to enter white collar and professional fields. And even the most old-fashioned parents wouldn't think of choosing a husband for a daughter who was out in the world, earning her living as a typist or schoolteacher.

At the same time, the dividing line which had once been sharply drawn between the Jews from Germany and those from Eastern Europe began to blur, and eventually disappeared. In a country where most people are of mixed national origins and where an aristocracy in the European sense doesn't exist, it matters little after a while if one's grandfather had been a shoemaker in Kovno, one's great-grandfather a merchant in Frankfurt, or one's many-times great-grandfather a physician in Cordoba.

SPORTS

Young Jews who wanted to make a living with their fists or pitching arms found wide opportunities in the early years of the century. Jewish athletes leaned particularly to boxing and baseball, two sports that required little money and no social status to undertake. Kid Kaplan and Benny Leonard, the lightweight champion from 1917 to 1924, were two of the world's best boxers in that or any era. Barney Ross, a champ in two divisions, fought and beat all comers in the 1930's, and in World War II battled his way to an equally distinguished combat record. Many Jewish baseball players made the big leagues in the 1920's and 1930's. The best was Hank Greenberg, who learned to hit on the streets of the Bronx. Greenberg, now a baseball executive, hit 58 homers in 1938, just two short of Babe Ruth's magic 60. Al (Flip) Rosen of the Cleveland Indians was the best known Jewish ballplayer of the 1950's, and Sandy Koufax, a Brooklyn boy, was the most feared pitcher in all of baseball during the 1960's. Jews excelled in other sports too. In basketball there was Nat Holman, the great player and coach. In football Benny Friedman of Michigan and Sid Luckman of Columbia College and the Chicago Bears were elected to the College Football Hall of Fame.

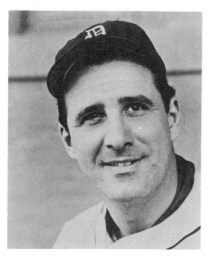

Hank Greenberg played first base for the Detroit Tigers from 1933 to 1946.

Sandy Koufax pitched for the Brooklyn and Los Angeles Dodgers from 1955 to 1966.

2. *Setbacks*

End of Immigration

For 300 years America had maintained an open-door policy toward European immigration. When 16 million people arrived from Europe within three or four decades, this policy began to be questioned. Labor objected on the ground that the immigrants threatened their jobs. The white-collar urban people had a vision of the cities being filled with slums. Farmers and small-town people in the West and South heard demagogues who assured them that pure white Anglo-Saxon America was being swallowed up by the "inferior" people from Southern and Eastern Europe. After the 1917 Russian Revolution, a hysteria swept the country, and every immigrant was suspected of carrying a bomb in his pocket. The United States Congress began passing anti-immigration acts culminating in the 1924 Johnson Bill which provided that only 2% of each nationality group be admitted each year. This percentage was based on the 1890 census when the large immigration waves had barely started. It practically put a stop to immigration from Southern and Eastern Europe. What Congress was saying, in effect, was that Italians, Slavs, Jews (and later Orientals) were less desirable than the people of Northern Europe. This theory ran counter to the principles on which America had been founded. It aggravated many prejudices which already existed.

Anti-Semitism

We have spoken earlier of the medieval myth of the Jew. This myth had to a large extent died out in modern times. No reasonable person would believe, for instance, that the Jews had caused the influenza epidemic of 1919 by poisoning the water system. But in 1911 many people were led to believe that a Jew in Russia, Mendel Beiliss, had killed a Christian child and used his blood for baking the Passover matzos. And at the turn of the century the Dreyfus case in France had rocked the world on both sides of the Atlantic. A parallel case in America was the Leo Frank case of 1915 in Atlanta, Georgia. Leo Frank, a Jew and a northerner, owned a factory in Atlanta. He had been charged on flimsy evidence of having killed a 14-year-old girl. He was sentenced to death, but his case aroused so much indignation all over the country, that the governor commuted the death sentence to imprisonment. Incensed by this commutation of the death sentence, a mob dragged Leo Frank out of prison and lynched him in Marietta, Georgia.

Social Justice, October 3, 1938. Father Coughlin's paper was barred from the mails for violation of the Espionage Act and ceased publication in 1942.

Modern anti-Semitism was fed from many sources. In the late nineteenth and early twentieth century books were written on both sides of the Atlantic setting forth the theory of the superiority of Aryan or Nordic races. In the American Middle West in the 1890's a movement called Populism arose among the farmers who were crying out for agrarian reforms. The Populists had a genuine grievance, but they believed that a conspiracy had been hatched against them in the big cities — New York and London — by "Jewish and English bankers." Their standard-bearer and hero was William Jennings Bryan, who in the 1896 election campaign made his famous "Cross of Gold" speech. This speech seemed to invoke an ancient image which linked the crucifixion and betrayal of Christ with the betrayal of the farmer by the "gold" or big money interests. The fact that at the time millions of Jews in this country were literally "Jews without money" had little influence on the popular mind.

In the 1920's anti-Semitism took on a more concrete form. Henry Ford published in his paper, *The Dearborn Independent*, a series of articles under the title of "The International Jew." These were supposed to be a transcript of a document known as "The Protocols of the Elders of Zion." This document had a curious history. It had first been "discovered" and publicized at the turn of the century in Russia by the Czar's secret police. It was supposed to be the transactions of a group called "The Elders of Zion," who had met in Prague and had plotted to take over the governments of the world with the help of corrupt politicians, Freemasons, liberals, and atheists. There

Father Charles Coughlin was pastor of the Shrine of the Little Flower at Royal Oak, Michigan, from 1926 until 1966. During the 1930's his radio sermons became increasingly political and anti-Semitic.

had never been such a group or such a conspiracy. The document was declared to be a forgery by several courts, in America and then in Switzerland where it was used in 1935 by Nazi agents. Henry Ford had to disclaim it at last; it was revived briefly by the Ku Klux Klan and again discredited. But like all forgeries or daring libels, it left an aura of ugly suspicion.

Between 1920 and 1930 the Ku Klux Klan, which began in the reconstruction days after the Civil War, was revived and this time the Klan attacked Negroes, Catholics, and Jews. In the 1930's after the stock market crash had brought on a severe economic depression, various crackpot organizations and individuals came forward. Father Coughlin, a Catholic priest, in his newspaper *Social Justice* and in weekly radio broadcasts blamed the ills of society on "international Jewish bankers and radicals." He was eventually silenced by the Church itself.

In those years discrimination was practiced against Jews in housing and employment. Many companies made no secret of the fact that they didn't hire Jews. Certain neighborhoods were restricted to Jews who wanted to rent or buy homes. Many universities and colleges adopted a quota system which limited the number of Jewish students to a certain percentage.

Hitler's rise to power in Germany and his attacks against the Jews had their echoes in America. The German-American Bund with Fritz Kuhn at its head held meetings that were a replica on a smaller scale

Supreme Court justices **Louis D. Brandeis** (1856-1941) and **Benjamin Cardozo** (1870-1938) were liberal jurists who based their interpretation of law upon social change. Brandeis served on the Court from 1916 to 1939, Cardozo from 1932 to 1938.

of anti-Jewish meetings in Nazi Germany. Local hate groups sprang up as well, such as William Dudley Pelley's Silver Shirts, which patterned itself on the fascist Black Shirts and the Nazi Brown Shirts. They made speeches, circulated anti-Semitic books and pamphlets, and looked to their local "fuehrers" to start a real assault on the Jews. When President Roosevelt initiated The New Deal he was attacked by these hate groups as well as by his political opponents, who made much of the fact that some of his advisers, or Brain Trust, happened to be Jews. Some of the more abusive attacks on the President had anti-Semitic overtones.

Justice **Felix Frankfurter** (1882-1965), born in Vienna, came to the United States in 1894. He was a professor of law at Harvard when Franklin Roosevelt appointed him to the Court in 1939. Frankfurter retired in 1962. Since then, Arthur Goldberg and Abe Fortas have served on the Court.

83

The attack on Pearl Harbor and the declaration of war on Nazi Germany dispersed the local Nazi groups and dealt a most effective blow against organized anti-Semitism. Jews in all walks of life fought in the war along with Americans of every national origin—including German and Japanese. When the war ended in 1945 and the enormity of what Hitler had done to the Jews of Germany and the German-occupied countries became known, a feeling of revulsion against Nazi ideas and methods turned the tide of anti-Semitism. Six million Jews had been killed or exterminated in Nazi death camps. The realization that anti-Semitism could be carried to such a conclusion in modern times shocked the American people. Political as well as Jewish exiles from Germany and Eastern Europe had come to the United States before the war. Under the Displaced Persons Act of 1948, 72,000 Jews were admitted after the war. Among them were scientists, scholars, and artists, as well as people of other skills who had been able to survive the concentration camps. For the most part they found America to be the refuge she had been since the day old Peter Stuyvesant agreed to allow the first 23 Jews to land in New Amsterdam.

After the Germans took Warsaw in 1939, they packed 500,000 Jews into a walled ghetto within the Jewish quarter of the city. In 1942-43 (above) large numbers were deported to death camps. A ghetto uprising broke out on April 19, 1943. It ended a month later when Germans demolished the ghetto.

Jewish Population of American Cities

New York City	1,836,000
Los Angeles	535,000*
Philadelphia	330,000*
Chicago	270,000*
Boston	175,000*
Newark	100,000
Miami	140,000
Washington, D.C.	100,000*
Baltimore	100,000
Cleveland	85,000
Detroit	85,000
San Francisco	73,000*
St. Louis	57,000

*greater area

(Estimated 1971 figures, Jewish Statistical Bureau)

3. *Statistics*

Out of an estimated 14 million Jews in the world today, 5.8 million live in the United States. If we looked at the distribution of the remaining 7.2 million, we would see that the United States has the largest number of Jews of any country in the world. In a total population of 204 million their percentage is 2.8%. This is not a large percentage — less than 3 out of 100; but with the exception of Israel, this is the largest percentage of any country in the world.

The reasons for the dramatic shift of Jewish population from Europe to America are not hard to find. The first is the large waves of immigration that took place in the nineteenth and early twentieth centuries. The second is the destruction of European Jews by the Nazis prior to and including World War II. The third reason lies in the nature of the American experience. For the first time in the long history of their wanderings the Jews found a country in which they did not have to court the favor of kings and autocratic governments. In America they could live as free individuals and not as a people apart. At the same time they have not had to submerge their identity or to give up their cultural heritage. Indeed this heritage, part of which was handed down from ancient times and part of which they acquired in the various lands of the diaspora, or exile, has played an important part in shaping American culture.

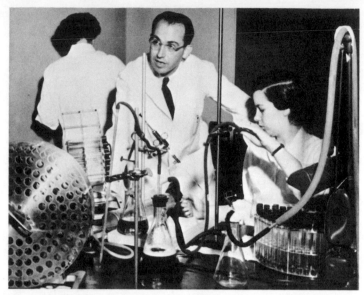

Dr. Jonas Salk developed the Salk antipolio vaccine in the Virus Research Laboratory at the University of Pittsburgh. Here, Salk inspects the work of a research assistant as she draws fluid from culture tubes.

4. *Science*

From the earliest times the Jews have valued the art of healing. Before medicine became the science it is today, there were Jewish doctors at the courts of kings, and two of the Marranos with Columbus were doctors. Today there are Jewish doctors in every branch of medical practice, on the teaching staffs of medical colleges, and in research laboratories throughout the country. In medicine the names of diseases or their cures are often associated with the names of the scientists who have discovered these diseases or their cures. Salk polio vaccine is named for Dr. Jonas Salk who developed the first vaccine which gives 98% immunity to paralytic poliomyelitis. Flexner B Dysentery was named for Dr. Simon Flexner of the Rockefeller Foundation who isolated the bacillus of that disease in 1889. He also made experimental studies of diphtheria toxins and is noted for discovery of serum treatment of spinal meningitis.

A Jewish doctor who pioneered in preventive medicine was Joseph Goldberger (1874-1929). He was born in Austria and brought to this country at the age of six. He graduated from Bellevue Hospital Medical

School in New York. In 1899 he entered the U.S. Public Health Service and was sent to Cuba and Mexico where he studied yellow fever and typhus, often using himself as a guinea pig. Between 1913 and 1925 he made a study of pellagra among the poor whites and Negroes in the South. It was thought at that time that pellagra was caused by a disease germ. Dr. Goldberger demonstrated that this disease was caused by the poor diet of the people of the South. His findings laid the basis for the modern science of nutrition.

Dr. Selman A. Waksman, working with a team of research scientists in soil chemistry at the New Jersey Agricultural Experiment Station, isolated streptomycin, the second antibiotic, the first being penicillin. It was he who named this and similar substances *antibiotics*. Streptomycin is effective against many diseases, but especially against tuberculosis. Its use has revolutionized the treatment of that once almost fatal disease. For this discovery and for subsequent work with other antibiotics Dr. Waksman received the Nobel Prize in Physiology and Medicine in 1952.

In 1921 the Nobel Prize for Physics was awarded to Albert Einstein. Einstein, whose theory of relativity is considered the greatest single scientific discovery of modern times, was a German Jew, but he had gone to Switzerland as a young man and did most of his important scientific work there. In 1934 he came to America to head the school of mathematics in the Institute for Advanced Study at Princeton, New Jersey, where he taught and worked until his death.

Selman Waksman, professor emeritus of microbiology at Rutgers University.

Another Nobel Prize winner in Physics (1944) was I. I. Rabi who received the prize for his work in phenomena connected directly or indirectly with magnetic fields. Isador Isaac Rabi was born in Austria in 1898 and was brought to the United States as a child. He graduated from Cornell University and received his Ph.D. from Columbia University in 1927. He has been associated with Columbia University ever since, becoming in 1964 the first man with the title of University Professor, a professorship without departmental ties. During World War II he did research in the field of microwave radar. From 1946 to 1956 he was a member of the General Advisory Committee of the Atomic Energy Commission. He has done valuable research on the peaceful uses of atomic energy and originated the movement resulting in CERN at Geneva, an international laboratory for the study of high energy physics.

A number of American Jewish physicists have made a contribution to the study of atomic energy and to the development of the first atom bomb. The most prominent among them was J. Robert Oppenheimer, who directed the Los Alamos laboratory where the first atom bomb was developed.

Albert Einstein (1879-1955) came to America in 1934. He had been director of theoretical physics at the Kaiser Wilhelm Institute in Berlin from 1914 until 1933, when the Nazis took away his property, his position, and his German citizenship.

Robert Oppenheimer (1904-1967) was a great teacher as well as a noted physicist.

Oppenheimer was born in New York in 1904, the son of a textile manufacturer who had come from Germany in 1888. He graduated from Harvard in 1926, and later studied at Cambridge University, England, and Gottingen, Germany. Between 1929 and 1947 he taught at the University of California and at Cal Tech and did research in theoretical physics. His interests extended beyond science to literature and the arts, but he did not become interested in economics and politics until about 1936. Then the events in Nazi Germany — Hitler's persecution of Jews — and the depression in this country (which made it hard for many of his students to find jobs) deeply disturbed him. During this period many intellectuals, scientists, and artists were also disturbed and took part in left-wing political movements. Though Oppenheimer did not join any political party, he had friends who did, and for this "guilt by association" he was to suffer later.

Meanwhile Oppenheimer was doing research in atomic energy. In 1943 he was appointed director of the Los Alamos, New Mexico, laboratory and headed a team of scientists and technicians who succeeded in exploding the first atom bomb. After the war, from 1947 to 1952, he was chairman of the General Advisory Council of the Atomic Energy Commission. Along with several other scientists he refused to work on the hydrogen bomb.

In December 1953 the AEC decided to review his loyalty status. In April 1954 his case was reviewed and he was cleared of charges of disloyalty, but was not given complete security clearance and was not allowed to continue to work on the AEC. Oppenheimer, who was director of the Institute for Advanced Study at Princeton, worked there until shortly before his death in 1967. In December 1963 Oppenheimer's contributions to science were acknowledged, and at the same time some restitution was made to him for the slur of the decade before, when he received the Fermi Award of $50,000, the Atomic Energy Commission's highest public award.

GOVERNMENT

During the presidency of Franklin Roosevelt, a number of administrative and advisory positions were held by Jews. Roosevelt's friend and neighbor from New York State, Henry Morgenthau, Jr., served as Secretary of the Treasury. Morgenthau initiated the successful wartime drive for Victory Bonds and was an advocate of worldwide monetary reform. David Lilienthal was a director and chairman of the Tennessee Valley Authority and in 1947 became the first chairman of the Atomic Energy Commission. Anna Rosenberg, an expert in labor and personnel relations, held positions with several government agencies during the New Deal years, and was Assistant Secretary of Defense in the Truman administration, from 1950 to 1953. Financier Bernard Baruch acted as an advisor on economics and national defense to every President from Woodrow Wilson to John F. Kennedy.

In 1932, Democrat Herbert Lehman followed Franklin Roosevelt as governor of New York. He served until 1942, and in 1949 was elected to the United States Senate. Lehman remained active in politics after his retirement in 1956, leading a reform movement within the Democratic party of New York City. Another Democrat, Ernest Gruening, was appointed governor of the Alaska territory in 1939. He campaigned for statehood and served as one of Alaska's first Senators, from 1959 to 1968. In 1961 President Kennedy appointed Governor Abraham Ribicoff of Connecticut to his Cabinet, as Secretary of Health, Education, and Welfare. Ribicoff was elected to the United States Senate in 1962 and re-elected in 1968. Jacob Javits of New York, a leader among liberal Republicans, entered the Senate in 1957 and was elected to a third term in 1968.

A noted Chicago labor lawyer, Arthur Goldberg, was Secretary of Labor under President Kennedy. He became an associate justice of the Supreme Court in 1962 and was ambassador to the United Nations from 1965 until 1968.

During the administration of Richard M. Nixon, Henry Kissinger, a German-born scholar and writer, served as an influential foreign policy adviser. In 1973, Kissinger was appointed Secretary of State.

5. *Business and Industry*

American Jews have been prominent in two industries (besides the retailing and garment industries already mentioned)—publishing and entertainment. There is still a Yiddish language press, though its reading public has dwindled. Several book publishers specialize in Yiddish and Hebrew books as well as English language books oriented toward the Jewish reader. The oldest of these is the Bloch Publishing Company, founded in 1854 in Cincinnati by Edward Bloch and Rabbi Isaac Wise. From Cincinnati it moved to Chicago, and then to New York. The Jewish Publication Society, established in Philadelphia in 1888, succeeded an earlier company founded in 1854.

In the last 30 or 40 years, however, Jews have entered in great numbers into the general American publishing field. Among them, Alfred Knopf is distinguished especially in publishing foreign authors in this country.

In the late nineteenth century several newspapers were rescued and given new life by two noted publishers. Joseph Pulitzer (1847-1911), half-Jewish, came to America from Hungary in 1864. He combined two papers to form the *St. Louis Post-Dispatch,* then moved on to the *New York World.* Before his death he established a school of journalism at Columbia University and endowed the Pulitzer prizes which have been awarded since 1917. His family still publishes the *Post-Dispatch.* In 1896 Adolph Ochs (1858-1935) went to New York from Chattanooga, Tennessee; he became the publisher of *The New York Times,* then on the verge of bankruptcy, and developed it into one of the world's greatest newspapers.

In the American theatre, a succession of notable producers has followed David Belasco's work at the turn of the century: Lee Shubert, Jed Harris, Herman Shumlin, and others. Shubert and his brothers managed and built theatres, staged operettas, and originated the modern musical revue. Shubert Alley remains a familiar spot in the New York theatre district.

Jews were pioneers in the movie industry. Adolph Zukor's career began in a penny arcade in 1903. Impressed by the popularity of imported French films, he formed his own company, Famous Players, and produced some of the earliest multi-reel feature length films. As an independent producer, he was given financial backing by Paramount Pictures, and later became president of Paramount. The four Warner

David Belasco (1853-1931), an innovator in the American theatre, came from San Francisco to New York as a stage manager in 1882 and by 1895 was guiding his own productions. Belasco wrote and directed plays, picked stars, designed sets. A master of elaborate stage effects, he specialized in storms.

brothers began making films in the early twenties. Public interest in movies was waning by the mid-twenties and the Warners made a desperate move to win back audiences. *Don Juan* in 1926 had a musical sound track, and in 1927 they released *The Jazz Singer*, considered to be the first talking picture, though it had little audible dialogue beyond the songs of Al Jolson. In July 1928 another Warner film, *The Lights of New York,* was the first full-dialogue release.

A series of mergers led to the formation of Metro-Goldwyn-Mayer in 1924. The Goldwyn and Metro companies had combined and were on the verge of bankruptcy when they joined forces with producers Louis B. Mayer and Irving Thalberg. Mayer, who had once been a scrap merchant, became one of Hollywood's flamboyant tycoons, and eventually headed the M-G-M company. Thalberg's career was short but brilliant. He had grown up in Brooklyn, and entered the film industry as a young secretary in the New York offices of Universal Pictures. His boss, Carl Laemmle, took him to Hollywood, where he learned production and rose quickly, hence was known as a "boy wonder." Sensitive to public taste, Thalberg was a hard-working producer who took part in every aspect of film-making. During the thirties some of his best films were *The Barretts of Wimpole Street* (with his wife Norma Shearer in the role of Elizabeth Barrett), *Mutiny on the Bounty,* and *Romeo and Juliet.* He died in 1936 at the age 37. F. Scott Fitzgerald drew upon the personality and career of Thalberg when he wrote *The Last Tycoon,* a novel which Fitzgerald himself did not live to finish.

6. *Theatre and Films*

Theatre has two masks — tragedy and comedy. So many Jewish American actors and actresses have donned the mask of comedy that they are sometimes credited with having a corner on that branch of entertainment. This isn't quite true, of course. Comedy on the American stage has drawn heavily on the various ethnic groups — Irish, Italians, and others. The Jews have only contributed their share. From the zany antics of the four Marx brothers in the early films to the dead-pan humor of Jack Benny, from the comic impersonations of Sid Caesar in the early days of television to the trenchant wit of Mort Sahl and other stand-up comedians, they have made several generations of American audiences laugh, chuckle or smile.

Danny Kaye is a comic genius in the great tradition. He was born in 1913 in Brooklyn, New York, as David Daniel Kaminsky, the son of a tailor. His first performance is supposed to have been in a school play and the part he played was that of a watermelon seed. At 13 he joined the "Borscht circuit," a name given to the summer resorts in the Catskill Mountains which catered mainly to Jewish audiences from New York and the vicinity. From there he went on to a successful career on stage, screen, and television. His wife Sylvia Fine has written most of his acts.

Brooklyn was also the birthplace of Zero Mostel (Samuel Joseph Mostel) who was born in 1915. His father was a rabbi. Where did he find the name Zero? He hit upon it "from nothing," it is reported. He is both a comedian and a character actor. His plays have been *A Funny Thing Happened on the Way to the Forum*, *Rhinoceros*, and *Waiting for Godot.* He created the part of Tevye in the musical *Fiddler on the Roof.*

The Marx brothers: Groucho, Harpo, and Chico.

Fanny Brice (1891-1951), a New Yorker, got her first big break in the Ziegfield Follies of 1910. A comic, singer, and mimic, she appeared in revues through the 1930's. Radio audiences knew her as Baby Snooks (above).

Brooklyn-born actor **Eli Wallach** co-starred with Zero Mostel in *Rhinoceros,* and with his wife Anne Jackson in *The Typists* and *The Tiger* (1963) and *Luv* (1964).

Actress and singer **Barbra Streisand** won an Oscar for her portrayal of Fanny Brice in the film *Funny Girl,* a musical based on the life of the famous entertainer.

Zero Mostel appeared in the stage and screen versions of *A Funny Thing Happened on the Way to the Forum.*

Judy Holliday won an Academy Award in 1950 for *Born Yesterday,* recreating a role she had originated on Broadway. She made the gum-chewing blond, Billie Dawn, not only funny but also human and moving, according to an article in the *New York Times* at the time of her death in 1965. Her acting career had started at the Village Vanguard with a group called the Revuers which included Adolph Green and Betty Comden. Comden and Green later wrote the play *Bells Are Ringing* which starred Judy Holliday in both stage and screen productions.

Another Oscar-winner, Shelley Winters, was named best supporting actress of 1959 for the part of Mrs. Van Daan in *The Diary of Anne Frank.* Actors Lee J. Cobb and Howard da Silva have had long careers on stage and in films and television. Cobb created the role of Willie Loman in Arthur Miller's *Death of a Salesman.* Da Silva, who directed and appeared in *The World of Sholom Aleichem* (1953) is perhaps best known for his roles in *Oklahoma!* and *Fiorello!* Most audiences are familiar with the work of Edward G. Robinson and Kirk Douglas, as well as with a new generation of performers — Barbra Streisand, actor-director Mike Nichols, Elaine May, George Segal, and singers Bob Dylan and Simon and Garfunkel.

7. *Music*

There is a story by Sholom Aleichem called "The Fiddle" about a boy who passionately loves music and wants above all else in the world to learn to play the fiddle. He knows that his prosperous, respectable father would never allow this, because to his father musicians are a ragged, disreputable lot who scrape away on their instruments at weddings and in country taverns. The boy goes to the sod-roofed hut of one of these village musicians and arranges to get fiddle lessons in secret. He is treated to a concert by the family orchestra of ragamuffins who play every kind of instrument including some home-made ones. The boy is also treated to a long and involved lecture "on music in general and fiddle-playing in particular" by the orchestra leader, a man named Naftalzi Bezborodka (*Bezborodka* means beardless). Carried away by his own eloquence, the village fiddler concludes, "The first fiddler in the world was Tubal Cain or Methuselah, I am not sure which....The second fiddler was King David. The third, a man named Paganini, also a Jew. The best fiddlers have always been Jews."

Pianist **Artur Rubinstein,** born in Poland in 1887, is considered one of the finest interpreters of Chopin.

A comic and touching boast, it was intended as irony in the context of the story. But this boast had a curiously prophetic ring. In the "lost" villages of the Russian Pale, during the latter part of the nineteenth century, village fiddlers were looked down upon, and boys like the hero of this story had to give up their dream of learning the fiddle. But in the next generation young people with musical talent were to be trained in the finest Russian conservatories and were to emerge as the great violin virtuosos of our time. Among them were Mischa Elman, Jascha Heifetz, and Nathan Milstein, all of whom later adopted America as their country. There were also pianists, and conductors. Still later came the American-born generation of Jewish musicians, singers, and composers of theatre music.

From *Watch Your Step* to *On Your Toes* and *Lady Be Good!* to *My Fair Lady,* the work of American Jewish composers and lyricists has run the full range of twentieth-century musical theatre. Critics and historians consider the musical comedy a distinctive American art form and trace its development from the operetta, variety show, and revue; they note the gradual integration of song and story, as well as the influence of jazz in the twenties and ballet in the thirties. Songs from the musical theatre form a kind of track through the American mind: the best songs catch the tone (or set the tone) of the year, and continue to be sung, whistled, even recorded long after the plays have closed. Irving Berlin, Jerome Kern, George Gershwin, Richard Rodgers

Jascha Heifetz, born in Lithuania in 1901, studied with his father before entering the St. Petersburg Conservatory in 1910. Unlike most child prodigies, he became even greater as an adult performer.

(with Lorenz Hart and Oscar Hammerstein), Frederick Loewe (with Alan Jay Lerner), and Leonard Bernstein are perhaps the best known of the Jewish composers for Broadway theatre.

One of the most haunting theatre songs, "Mack the Knife," is from an off-Broadway play, *The Threepenny Opera,* and is the result of an unusual collaboration. Its composer Kurt Weill came to America in 1935, two years after leaving Nazi Germany. *Threepenny* (with text by German playwright Bertolt Brecht) had opened in 1928 at a small theatre in Berlin. It ran for five years and was popular throughout Europe during the thirties. Although it appeared briefly on Broadway

Tenors **Richard Tucker** (left) and **Jan Peerce.** Tucker was a cantor at the Brooklyn Jewish Center before his debut with the Metropolitan Opera in 1945. Peerce first appeared at the Met in 1941, as Alfredo in *La Traviata.*

George Gershwin (1898-1937) first played *Rhapsody in Blue* with Paul Whiteman's orchestra in 1924—the same year that *Lady Be Good!* opened on Broadway. His use of jazz rhythms marked a turning point in American music. Most of Gershwin's lyrics were written by his brother Ira.

in 1933, nearly 20 years were to pass before American audiences would see an effective English version of the play.

Weill remained in America for the rest of his life, and composed a number of fine scores for the Amerian musical theatre—*Knickerbocker Holiday, Lady in the Dark, Lost in the Stars*. In 1950 Marc Blitzstein showed him a translation he had made of one of the songs from *Threepenny*, which he had seen as a student in Germany. After Weill's death, Blitzstein, a notable composer and lyricist in his own right, went ahead and made a brilliant adaptation of the text and the remaining songs. *Threepenny Opera* began its long off-Broadway run in March 1954. Since then it has also been staged by many civic theatres and colleges.

Leonard Bernstein, music director of the New York Philharmonic from 1958 to 1969, was the first American-born and -trained conductor to hold that post. A pianist, teacher, and composer, Bernstein's scores include *On the Town, Wonderful Town,* and *West Side Story.*

Sculptor **Seymour Lipton** works chiefly in sheet metal with textured overlays of molten bronze. His pieces combine mechanical and natural forms.

8. *Art*

In 1905 a young American artist named Max Weber arrived in Paris. This was a momentous year in the history of art, for in that year Cezanne, Matisse, and other modern French painters, who had been turned down by the staid French Academy of Art, held their first public exhibitions at the now famous Autumn Salon. Weber remained in Paris for three years and studied with Henri Matisse. When he returned to America he brought with him the concepts and techniques in painting which were considered revolutionary at the time, but which have since become accepted and have influenced modern art, both abstract and representational.

Max Weber (1881-1961) was the son of Russian-Jewish immigrant parents who had come to America when he was 10 years old. Like most immigrants, his family was poor, but he managed to study art at the Pratt Institute in Brooklyn before going to Paris. In his early paintings based on New York scenes he demonstrated a free and dynamic use of form and color. His painting *Chinese Restaurant* (1915), owned by the Whitney Museum of American Art, is often reproduced as an example of American abstract art. Later in his career Weber's work became representational and he turned for subjects to his

Jewish background. Examples of this work are *The Hasidic Dance* and *Adoration of the Moon.* The latter is derived from an old Jewish ceremony in which 10 men at the close of the Sabbath gather in the courtyard of the synagogue to bless the rising moon when its light is the strongest.

Mark Rothko (1903-1970), an abstract painter, was at one time a student of Weber's. Rothko was born in Russia and grew up in Oregon. His paintings hang in the Whitney, the Museum of Modern Art, and the Chicago Art Institute.

Emphatic in his opposition to abstract art, Aaron Bohrod derives from the regional school of American painters. Born and raised in Chicago, he has said that he wanted to do for Chicago what John Sloan had done for New York — that is, paint city streets, houses, railroads — whether they were conventionally beautiful or not. He has done this with success. Appointed artist in residence at the University of Wisconsin he has painted the towns and countryside of the Middle West, as well as scenes from the West and South. In recent years he has done striking still life paintings, and worked on pottery and textile design.

Represented at the Whitney, the Museum of Modern Art, and other leading American art galleries are Hyman Bloom and Jack Levine, both of Boston. Expressionist in technique, their paintings are rich in texture, brilliant in color. Bloom has used Jewish subjects of cantors,

Alfred Stieglitz (1864-1946), photographer and art dealer, opened the Photo-Secession Gallery at 291 Fifth Avenue in 1906. At "291" Stieglitz exhibited for the first time in America the work of Matisse and other modern French and American painters.

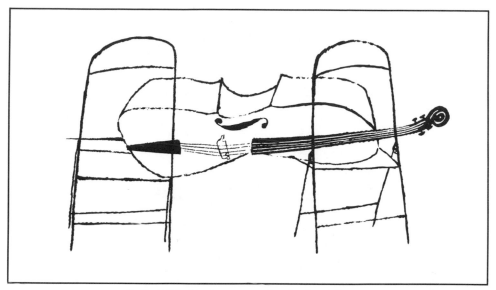

Cello With Chairs, a drawing by Ben Shahn.

rabbis, synagogue interiors. Jack Levine's paintings are satiric in subject matter, close to caricature. He paints groups of people to illustrate avarice, greed, and violence in modern society. Two examples often reproduced are *Gangster's Funeral* (1952) and *Military Symphony* (1962).

Ben Shahn (1898-1969) was an artist of remarkable range and versatility, whose work included fresco murals, oil paintings, and water colors, as well as posters and book and magazine illustrations. The son of a carpenter, he was born in Russia and was brought to New York at the age of eight. As a young boy in Brooklyn playing with neighborhood kids he did sidewalk chalk drawings of the sports heroes of the day. He attended high school at night and worked during the day as a lithographer's apprentice. His work as a lithographer gave him a thorough knowledge of draughtmanship and a respect for art as a *craft*. One of the first books he illustrated was a *Haggadah,* the Hebrew book of the Passover service. In the 1930's and 1940's he, along with many artists, worked for the Federal Arts Project. He made fresco murals for government buildings—the Bronx Central Annex Post Office, the Federal Security Building in Washington, and a housing development for garment workers in Roosevelt, New Jersey. This last mural is a series of panels depicting the history of American immigrants.

In his later work Shahn used symbol and allegory. These are evident in a group of paintings called "The Lucky Dragon" which he developed from some drawings he had done for a magazine article about a Japanese fishing trawler, *The Lucky Dragon*. In the article, physicist Ralph Lapp described the fate of the trawler, which was covered with radioactive dust from a hydrogen bomb test at Bikini Atoll. The crew became sick and one man died after long illness.

Wedding dance — a scene from the M-G-M film
The Fixer, based on Bernard Malamud's novel.

9. *Literature*

In 1966 two books came out almost simultaneously, one of them a novel, the other a historical account, on the same theme. The novel was *The Fixer* by Bernard Malamud; the historical account was *Blood Accusation: The Strange History of the Beiliss Case* by Maurice Samuel. Both of these books were widely read and favorably received by the critics. That they should win praise for their literary merit is understandable. Bernard Malamud is one of the leading novelists writing in America today; Maurice Samuel, who died in 1972, was a distinguished scholar and writer on subjects pertaining to Judaism. That the

Twenty years after publication of his World War II novel *The Naked and the Dead*, **Norman Mailer** wrote *The Armies of the Night*, a vivid account of the October 1967 march on the Pentagon to protest the war in Vietnam. Mailer continued to examine aspects of American life in such books as *Miami and the Siege of Chicago* (1968) and *Marilyn* (1973), a biography of actress Marilyn Monroe.

theme of these two books — the court trial of an obscure Jew in Czarist Russia over 50 years ago — should capture the interest of the American reading public is a cause for wonder. The wonder is dispelled when we realize the importance and growing popularity of Jewish subjects and of books with Jewish background in the world today. The Nobel Prize for literature in 1966 was shared by two Jewish writers, S. Y. Agnon of Israel and Nellie Sachs of Sweden. But it is chiefly in America that books of Jewish interest are being published and read at an astonishing rate. This has been true since the end of World War II, and even more so in the last 10 or 15 years.

Why is this true? One reason is that American Jewish writers have become intensely aware of their heritage and have been rediscovering their own background as a rich source of material. Yet all of these books have not been written by Jews. *The Wall*, a novel about the heroic uprising in the Warsaw ghetto in 1943, was written by John Hersey. *The Source*, a novel which covers the whole panorama of Jewish history, is by James Michener, who first became known for his *Tales of the South Pacific*. The Jew in literature is no longer an exotic character. Neither is he a stereotype. Earlier books about Jews, like *What Makes Sammy Run* (1941) and *I Can Get It For You Wholesale* (1937) caricatured the self-seeking ambitious Jew. By contrast, Herbert Gold's *Fathers* (1966) probes more deeply and with greater sympathy into the motivations of a man with ambition and drive to succeed.

Saul Bellow's novels and stories reflect his Jewish background and his understanding of the Jewish-American character. He received National Book Awards for *The Adventures of Augie March* (1953) and *Herzog* (1964). His novel *Mr. Sammler's Planet* (1969) was also highly praised by critics.

In the short story, the character sketch, and the memoir, writers have captured the essence of growing up as the children of Jewish immigrants in America. Among these are Meyer Levin's *The Old Bunch,* Michael Gold's *Jews Without Money,* Charles Angoff's *When I Was a Boy in Boston,* Henry Roth's *Call It Sleep,* and Alfred Kazin's *A Walker in the City.* J. D. Salinger's stories about the Glass family have been especially interesting to young readers, and so has his novel, *Catcher in the Rye.* Philip Roth's novels, particularly *Goodbye, Columbus* and *Portnoy's Complaint,* have been both praised and criticized for their frank portrayals of Jewish life in the United States.

Jewish writers have not confined themselves to Jewish subjects. Ben Hecht, Robert Nathan, Nathanael West, Dorothy Parker, and Edna Ferber have written on a variety of themes, ranging from fantasy to satire to historical romance. Two of the best World War II novels were written by American Jews — *The Young Lions* by Irwin Shaw and *The Naked and the Dead* by Norman Mailer. In his recent books Mailer has used his skill as a novelist to write about current history. There are many American Jewish literary critics of note — Lionel Trilling, Irving Howe, Philip Rahv, Leslie Fiedler. Some of these men also teach literature in universities and colleges.

In the 1920's the American theatre was enlivened by playwrights of Jewish origin — George Kaufman, Moss Hart, S. N. Behrman, Elmer Rice, Sidney Kingsley. During the 1930's Clifford Odets wrote plays of social protest. *Awake and Sing* was about a Jewish family caught in the depression, *Golden Boy* about an Italian youth forced by poverty to turn from music to professional prizefighting. Odets's plays were produced by the Group Theatre of which Harold Clurman was one of the founders and directors. Clurman is one of the best drama critics writing today.

Lillian Hellman, a native of New Orleans, became known for her play *The Children's Hour* in 1935. She is best known for *The Little Foxes,* a play about the changing South, which became a film and an opera (*Regina,* with music by Marc Blitzstein). In 1969, Miss Hellman published an autobiographical book entitled *An Unfinished Woman.* She continued the account of her life and literary career in *Pentimento: A Book of Portraits,* which appeared in 1973.

One of the leading playwrights in America is Arthur Miller whose *Death of a Salesman,* first produced in 1949, has appeared throughout the world. His other plays include *All My Sons, The Crucible,* and *A View from the Bridge.* Miller has not dealt with Jewish characters or themes, but in *The Price* (1968) he introduced an old Jewish furniture dealer, a minor character who added depth and humor to the play.

A Jewish American writer of great power and originality, Edward Wallant, was born in New Haven, Connecticut, in 1926 and died in 1962 at the age of 36. He wrote four novels, two of which were published after his death. He wrote of submerged people, Jews and Italians in city ghettos. *The Pawnbroker* is about a Jew, Saul Nazerman, who

Isaac Bashevis Singer came to New York from Poland in 1935. His short stories and novels, all written in Yiddish, have been translated into English. *Zlateh the Goat,* his first children's book, is a collection of stories drawn from Jewish folklore.

105

had been a university professor in Poland, saw his wife and two children killed in a Nazi concentration camp, and then managed to escape to America. He became a pawnbroker in Harlem. The novel, and the film based on it, is a modern fable with terrifying implications. A man deprived of his humanity—of everything he cares for in life—turns into a lifeless automaton. He treats the derelicts and the poor who come to him—the Puerto Ricans and Negroes—with cruel indifference. When violence erupts and his young Puerto Rican assistant gets killed in trying to save him, the pawnbroker is at last able to feel pain. Though it is too late to undo the harm he has caused, he is a human being once more.

Awake and Sing! Act II, scene I from the Group Theatre production of Clifford Odets's play, 1935. Onstage (left to right): actors John Garfield, Morris Carnovsky, J. Edward Bromberg, Stella and Luther Adler, Sanford Meisner, and Art Smith. The title of the play is from lines spoken by the grandfather (Morris Carnovsky), quoting the prophet Isaiah: "Awake and sing, ye that dwell in dust, and the earth shall cast out the dead." (*Courtesy of the Theatre Collection, The New York Public Library at Lincoln Center*)

End of the Megillah

The Book of Esther in the Bible is called the Megillah. The word *Megillah* means Scroll in Hebrew. Once a year on the eve of the holiday of Purim, the Megillah is unrolled and the story of Queen Esther and of how she saved the Jews from destruction by their enemy, Haman, is read aloud. Since the listeners, especially the children, are impatient for the reading to be over and the holiday fun to begin, the word Megillah has come to mean in a figurative sense any long and detailed explanation or account. "Make it short, don't give me the whole megillah," storytellers are cautioned. The history of the Jews in America would indeed be a whole megillah, if it were told in detail. We have been brief, and so this particular megillah is over. But unlike the Book of Esther it isn't really finished. The history of the world, the history of America, and the history of the Jews in America is still going on.

...INDEX...

ABOUT THE AUTHOR...

FRANCES BUTWIN was born in Warsaw, Poland, and came to America in 1922 with her parents and younger brother and sister. They settled in Charleston, South Carolina, where she attended high school and graduated from the College of Charleston.

With her husband Julius, Mrs. Butwin translated from the Yiddish a collection of Sholom Aleichem's short stories, *The Old Country*. After her husband's death in 1945, she translated a second volume of Sholom Aleichem's stories, *Tevye's Daughters*, and his novel *Wandering Star*. The musical *Fiddler on the Roof* is based upon her translations.

Mrs. Butwin served as a librarian in the Literature and Language Department of the Minneapolis Public Library until her retirement in 1974. She lives in Minneapolis.

The IN AMERICA *Series*

The AMERICAN INDIAN *in America, Volume I*
The AMERICAN INDIAN *in America, Volume II*
The CHINESE *in America*
The CZECHS & SLOVAKS *in America*
The DUTCH *in America*
The EAST INDIANS & PAKISTANIS *in America*
The ENGLISH *in America*
The FRENCH *in America*
The GERMANS *in America*
The GREEKS *in America*
The HUNGARIANS *in America*
The IRISH *in America*
The ITALIANS *in America*
The JAPANESE *in America*
The JEWS *in America*
The MEXICANS *in America*
The NEGRO *in America*
The NORWEGIANS *in America*
The POLES *in America*
The PUERTO RICANS *in America*
The RUSSIANS *in America*
The SCOTS & SCOTCH-IRISH *in America*
The SWEDES *in America*
The UKRAINIANS *in America*
The FREEDOM OF THE PRESS *in America*
The FREEDOM OF RELIGION *in America*
The FREEDOM OF SPEECH *in America*

We specialize in publishing quality books for young people. For a complete list please write:

LERNER PUBLICATIONS COMPANY
241 First Avenue North, Minneapolis, Minnesota 55401